A MISSION
JOURNEY

A MISSION
JOURNEY

A HANDBOOK FOR
VOLUNTEERS

DISCIPLESHIP RESOURCES

P.O. BOX 340003 • NASHVILLE, TN 37203-0003
www.discipleshipresources.org

ISBNs
Print 978-0-88177-669-0
Mobi 978-0-88177-670-6
Epub 978-0-88177-671-3

Library of Congress Control Number: 2013949364

Printed in the United States of America

DR 669

CONTENTS

Foreword vii

Premise ix

Acknowledgments xi

Introduction xiii

PHASE ONE
SETTING THE CONTEXT FOR VOLUNTEER MISSION EXPERIENCES

Theology of Christian Mission 3

Expanding Cultural Awareness 11

Volunteer Mission Experiences and Spiritual Transformation 17

Christian Mission in a Time of Globalization 23

PHASE TWO
EXPANDING CULTURAL AWARENESS AND CULTIVATING SPIRITUAL TRANSFORMATION

Introduction 41

Living Our Faith in Mission: A Study on Luke 10 43

Engaging in Group Conversation 49

Spiritual Centering: A Handout for Participants 53

BEFORE the Mission Experience

Introduction 59

Answering God's Call 61

Search Me and Know My Heart 65

They Will Know We Are Christians by Our Love 75

Dedication Services for Volunteers and Hosts 81

DURING the Mission Experience

Introduction 87

A Meal Is More Than a Menu... 93

Answering God's Call 97

Search Me and Know My Heart 101

They Will Know We Are Christians by Our Love 113

AFTER the Mission Experience

Introduction 125

Answering God's Call 127

Search Me and Know My Heart 131

They Will Know We Are Christians by Our Love 135

Notes and Sources 139

Appendix

The Mission Theology statement guides Global Ministries' participation
    in the *Missio Dei*..145

Best Practices for UMVIM/VIM (Sending and Hosting) Teams 149

United Methodist Committee on Relief (UMCOR)
    Volunteers and US Response to Disaster 151

    Volunteers and International Disaster Response 155

    Global Health and Mission Volunteers 159

Introduction to In Mission Together: 50/50 Partnership Covenant......................163

Partnership Covenant 50/50..165

United Methodist Communications (UMCOM)
    Understanding Information and Communications Technology in the
        Developing World..167

Additional Recommended Resources....................................171

FOREWORD

It has been my pleasure to work with the global task force and writers to coordinate this handbook for volunteers in mission. Our goal was to create a handbook that would allow teams to work through and reflect on the general information needed to coordinate the sending and hosting of mission teams. We wanted to create a resource that was more than a how-to manual in the hope that it would help reenvision a new approach to engaging global volunteers in mission.

Approximately six million Americans engage in short-term missions domestically and internationally each year. The global mission of The United Methodist Church reflects teams and individuals organized for short-term mission not only from the United States but also from Central Conferences and through other church relationships. Both the United Methodist Volunteers In Mission (UMVIM) and international Volunteers In Mission (VIM) communities are vital to making each mission journey beneficial to sending and hosting teams. Members of both communities were part of the task force that helped develop this handbook.

We asked the task force and writers to consider the ways in which this handbook could be used by team leaders and team members, hosts and mission sites, and jurisdictional coordinators as they work to support the preparation of US teams, Global Ministries staff who support and are charged with oversight of the church's global mission, and UMVIM and VIM coordinators. The Mission Volunteers office provides training and networking with the UMVIM and International VIM coordinators.

The UMVIM Jurisdictional Coordinators and Conference Coordinators are mandated to train and mobilize volunteers for mission. They will be the main distributors of this handbook. Supporting their significant role, the Northeastern, North Central, and Southeastern Jurisdictions will offer accident and medical insurance to teams and individuals beginning in 2014.

We are in a new era of mission in which millions of people choose to engage in short-term mission and ministry outside large mission agencies, yet supported by the church. In response, UMVIM must provide opportunities and resources for training and support to equip those engaged in God's mission so that sending and hosting teams alike can be effective and prepared for their journey. This handbook is one vital tool for preparation and the future of meaningful partnerships.

Una Jones
Mission Volunteers
Assistant General Secretary

PREMISE

The leadership of UMVIM and VIM accepts the challenge and comes together in collaboration for the sake of equipping communities for mission. We do so respecting our cultures, having faith that through preparation we will recognize our common goal of following Christ. In service together we will share the love of Christ. We will build relationships, experience grace, and develop mutual trust. When we part company, we do so with the hope of a better future, reflecting on our experience together. We covenant to pray for one another, lifting prayers for transformation, justice, and change. We are better together than alone and can do all things through Christ who strengthens us.

ACKNOWLEDGMENTS

The original United Methodist Volunteers In Mission Training Manual was written by a task force of experienced team leaders to ensure the creation of a common document that could be used in team leader training. This handbook was developed by a variety of people from different backgrounds and areas of expertise for the same purpose. The project was forged in 2010, and the existing task force formed in 2011.

A group of passionate volunteers and mission-minded folks comprised the global task force. Among them were the United Methodist Volunteers In Mission Jurisdictional Coordinators, Global Ministries Mission Volunteers staff, international Volunteers In Mission hosts, and the writers who contributed to this handbook.

Una Jones, Assistant General Secretary of Mission Volunteers, and Jeanie Blankenbaker, consultant, served as editors for this project. We wish to thank everyone for their contributions, support, and guidance along the way.

We also wish to thank Lorna Jost (North Central Jurisdiction), Gregory Forrester (Northeastern Jurisdiction, now Assistant General Secretary for UMCOR US Disaster Response), Debbie Vest (South Central Jurisdiction), Paulette West (Southeastern Jurisdiction), Heather Wilson (Western Jurisdiction), Willie Berman (Global Ministries missionary in Mexico), Mike Collins (Western North Carolina Annual Conference), Josephine Deere (Oklahoma Indian Missionary Conference), Lynette Fields (Florida Annual Conference), Malcolm Frazier (Executive Secretary of Mission Volunteers, Global Ministries), Jana Krizova (Czech Republic), Kelvin Sauls, (California Pacific Annual Conference), and consultant Elizabeth Calvert.

Finally, we would like to express our gratitude to those who contributed to the writing and content of this handbook: Jeremy Basset, elmira Nazombe, Jane P. Ives, David Wildman, Gregory Forrester, Jack Amick, Shannon Trilli, Patrick Friday, and N. Neelley Hicks.

INTRODUCTION

A Mission Journey is a tool for teams to use as they prepare for mission journeys in the United States and around the world. We hope it will influence UMVIM and VIM communities to review their approach to volunteering. UMVIM is the most vibrant mission outreach program within The United Methodist Church, and as it continues to grow we want to offer this handbook as a tool for volunteers to reimagine their roles.

This handbook is for team leaders, team members, and others who will engage in short-term mission volunteer journeys. It encourages short-term mission volunteers to reflect on the reasons *why* they engage in mission and *how* they prepare to be more intentional to those they encounter on their journeys. *Presence* and *relationship* are emphasized throughout the book, along with the idea that each of these is more important than the actual work itself. One goal of this book is to help volunteers shape the stories of their mission experiences in a way that enhances their personal and spiritual journeys.

A mission *journey* as opposed to a mission *trip,* involves dialog, respect, and relationship building. Journeys are best planned by reflecting on past experiences, the lessons learned from those experiences, and the team leader resources that are available. Most of all, mission journeys require an invitation, flexibility, willingness to listen to your hosts and to follow their lead and direction, and an understanding that this is God's mission and not our own.

A Mission Journey is organized to help you explore the approach to your mission by examining each of the areas listed below.

Theology: This section explores *why* God calls us to engage in short-term mission. It urges us to ask ourselves if we are working *with* or *for* others, and if they are partners or recipients of our generosity. It also explores the need for interdependency.

Cultural Sensitivity: This section examines the dual responsibilities of hosting and sending teams. Each side must be intentional in its relationships with the other. As volunteers we must first understand ourselves and the intentions of our own culture and community before we attempt to understand the intentions of other cultures and communities.

Spirituality: Mission journeys can have a tremendous impact on our lives, and they are often transformational experiences. This requires our full participation BEFORE, DURING, and AFTER the mission journey. Our spirituality evolves over time. We can learn from one another, share our mission stories, and witness God's grace.

Peace and Justice: John Wesley reminds us that there are two approaches to God's mission: caring spiritually for others and ourselves and seeking justice. Seeking justice requires us to understand the context of our work beyond the tasks we will be performing. We are to be engaged not only in helping others with their immediate needs but also exploring the larger cause of those needs.

A Mission Journey guides participants through exercises related to and reflection in each of these areas BEFORE, DURING, and AFTER their mission journeys. It provides practical exercises, material for discernment, and encouragement for intentional dialog.

The introduction to Phase Two of this handbook provides a Bible study and two documents that suggest ways to deepen the experience of your team members. "Engaging in Group Conversation" (pages 49–51) offers suggestions you may use when your team meets, BEFORE, DURING, and AFTER the mission experience. Share "Spiritual Centering: A Handout for Participants" (pages 53–55) with other mission volunteers early in your life together. Although some of your team members may have already developed an active prayer life and have a deep spirituality, they will not all be at the same place in their spiritual journeys. During orientation discuss the importance of spiritual centering as a way to connect with the Holy Spirit, tune out distractions, make intentional decisions, and think about and respond to situations that trigger instinctive reactions. In addition to encouraging team members to select and practice a spiritual centering prompt, provide quiet time for them to do so.

The meditations provided for individual and/or group use in the BEFORE, DURING, and AFTER sections can help both hosts and visiting volunteers become like the "good soil" in the parable of the sower and the seed (Matt. 13:8)—open to the power of the Holy Spirit as they prepare for, engage deeply in, and meaningfully respond to their mission experiences. The team leader or spiritual guide may duplicate those pages for team members and should make sure members have notebooks or paper for journaling. If individuals use the devotional pages privately, be sure to schedule time for group processing and reflection, which are essential for maximum learning and spiritual growth. Invite different persons to read the scripture passages, the reflection input, and the reflection and response suggestions aloud before sharing their own thoughts.

The BEFORE section also provides ideas for dedication services for both hosts and volunteers, each within the context of their larger community (pages 81–83). The DURING section begins with "Tools for Cultivating Spiritual Transformation During a Mission Experience" and offers suggestions for both planned and spontaneous worship experiences. Weaving worship throughout the mission experience sets a spiritual context for all that happens, encourages a positive group attitude, and helps team members overcome rough spots.

The DURING section includes "Daily Reflection and Group Processing During a Mission Experience" (pages 90–92), which offers questions to use and insights about this vital part of a team's life together. This section also provides ideas for "Final Reflections, Closing Worship, and Preparation for Returning Home" (pages 119–121).

Both hosts and volunteer team leaders and spiritual guides will need to determine how to use the activities provided for AFTER the mission experience. Team reunions provide a good opportunity for thoughtful reflection and sharing. If distance makes it difficult for all members to reunite, the team leader and spiritual guide might suggest a time line for individual use of the meditations, followed by a group session whenever possible, perhaps as part of another gathering (such as an annual conference session or a mission awareness event). Skype and other online programs might help include those who could not otherwise participate, and the team leader and/or spiritual guide can follow up with participants individually, asking questions that prompt self-awareness and sharing along the lines of "How is it with your soul?"

The Appendix lists resources, including other devotional materials, from which to choose what you believe will best meet the needs of team members and fit the duration of your experience, type of project (housing rehab or other construction, disaster relief and recovery, medical, program leadership, or some combination of these), and location (local, national, international). It also provides additional information and resources for volunteers, including best practices before engaging in the outreach ministry of helping, supporting, and encouraging any particular mission. There is additional information about UMCOR's role in volunteer missions, including health care volunteers, the In Mission Together program, and additional resources and references for information and support.

Opportunities to study and meditate on scripture, formal and informal worship experiences, guided practice in spiritual centering, and group conversations will help cultivate spiritual transformation. When you lift up the Holy in the midst of ordinary events and provide opportunities for participants—volunteers and hosts alike—to connect more deeply with God and one another BEFORE, DURING, and AFTER a mission experience, you partner with God in the ongoing activity of creation.

Let the journey begin.

PHASE ONE

SETTING THE CONTEXT FOR
VOLUNTEER MISSION EXPERIENCES

THEOLOGY OF CHRISTIAN MISSION

Jeremy Basset

Our God is a missionary God; the Bible is a missionary document; the agent of God's mission is the Holy Spirit; the partner with this Spirit is the called-out community, the Church of Jesus Christ; and the work of this community of Christ-followers is to facilitate the coming of the kingdom of God in ways consistent with who Jesus is and what Jesus did.

God's kingdom is not to be confused with our fallible and often manipulative human kingdoms. God's kingdom is founded on a personal, loving relationship with the King (some prefer to use the word "kin-dom" to signify this wonderful truth). In this kingdom, God alone reigns, and we connect joyfully and equally with one another. There is no hierarchy, control, or exploitation. This is the world restored to the way God intended it to be. It is the reign of God alone!

SHARING CHRIST'S LOVE IN A BROKEN WORLD

When Jesus sends out seventy of his followers, it is an audacious and remarkable act (Luke 10:1-21). This is recorded early in Luke's Gospel and long before Jesus' death, resurrection, ascension, and Pentecost. He sent out these rookie disciples to participate in the work of God's mission with few tools, little experience and—let's be honest—an unclear understanding of what the kingdom they were to proclaim was all about!

What this motley group of Christ followers did was remarkable (Luke 10:17). Such has been the impact of ordinary disciples for over two thousand years. People, drawn to Jesus and recognizing in him one who has been sent by God to inaugurate something powerful and new, are then propelled, ready or not it seems, into the world to make a difference on behalf of this great cause—to proclaim God's reign and to connect with one another.

Many Volunteers In Mission leaders have been heard to say, "Our work is to share the love of Christ in ways that make a Christian difference." A grassroots movement,

3

its participants seem to echo the enthusiasm and commitment of those early disciples to share Jesus with a world in need.

Ordinary people have done extraordinary deeds when, connected to Christ, they engage the world on behalf of God's kingdom. The purpose of following Christ is to work on God's behalf.

A FAITH IN TWO MOVEMENTS

There are two inextricable strands of our faith in Christ. One draws us toward God and the other propels us toward the world. Missionary priest and seminary professor, Father Anthony Gittins, describes this in terms of a call or an encounter with God. This call or encounter is accompanied by a disturbance or displacement, a radical reordering of our lives that takes us out of a world centered on ourselves and refocuses us on God. We are sent out, "co-missioned" to live and serve in Jesus' name.[1] We are called to be sent!

In a similar vein, Elizabeth O'Connor, writing about the life and ministry of the Church of the Saviour in Washington, DC, notes that an authentic Christian life involves both an inward and an outward journey.[2] Commitment to God in Christ leads to an ever-deepening personal relationship with God as well as an ever-increasing involvement in the pain and brokenness of the world.

Love for God and love for God's world are inseparable. God's plan and purpose is to reshape the world according to its original design. Drawn into a personal relationship with God, we discover the depth of God's love for us and for the world. We are then propelled back into the world so that everyone might know of this great love.

Peter Storey notes that the verse quoted often from Revelation describing Jesus standing at the door and knocking (Rev. 3:20) implies a fellowship greater than just "Jesus and me." He notes that when we say yes to Jesus, he responds, "Can I bring my friends too?"[3] A connection to Christ is a connection to a broken world.

GOD'S MISSION AT THE HEART OF SCRIPTURE

The mission of God in essence is what the Bible is all about. This is the grand narrative of scripture.[4] God's mission is what holds the threads of the Hebrew scriptures and New Testament together.

The Bible was redacted into its present form by a group of editors and authors who were guided by the Holy Spirit and who chose from a rich and diverse collection of books, stories, poems, and letters, commending to us sixty-six books and leaving out others. What informed their choice? To understand this, we need to first understand how the authors of scripture perceived who God was and what God was doing in the world. Woven throughout the various literary forms that comprise the Bible is the theme that our Creator God is at work in the world bringing about God's reign.

Our God is a missionary God. This is God's nature and not only a characteristic of God. Having created us and set the world in motion, we undermined the purpose of our creation—living in fellowship with God—by our self-centered ways. Rather than abandoning the human project as a wasted endeavor, God continues to restore humanity to God's original plan.

God the Missionary has used many people in support of this work: individual leaders, prophets, priests, and even kings, in addition to the many people called to serve as witnesses to God's cause.

The pinnacle of God's work is Jesus—God made flesh, living among us in service of God's mission. Jesus spoke about, demonstrated with signs and wonders, and lived solely for the establishment of God's kingdom. After Jesus' death, resurrection, and ascension, God inaugurated the age of the Holy Spirit (already at work throughout the Hebrew scriptures but now available to all) as a sign that God will work through anyone and everyone who devote their lives to the service of God's kingdom.

Since then, God's mission has been at the heart of the church of Jesus Christ. Therefore, it is not so much that the church has a mission, but that God's mission has a church. The primary agent of God's mission is the Holy Spirit, and the Holy Spirit needs a human partner. The Holy Spirit's partner is the church. Yes, individuals are filled and empowered by the Holy Spirit; but if you look carefully, you will see that the gifts and the fruit of the Spirit flourish best in the shared, corporate life of the body of Christ.

FOLLOWING JESUS TO THE MARGINS

The purpose of devoting our lives to following Christ is not to sit around waiting for the return of Jesus. Rather, our faith is defined by our active, intentional, and Christlike participation in the work of God's mission. We must share our faith. We are meant to be devoted to following Christ out into the world. Our witness should conform to the life and example of the One we follow.

A United Methodist Church in Jackson, Mississippi, has as its mission statement ". . . revealing heaven on earth."[5] The obvious implication of this is that we need to live and serve in such a way that we represent God's mission well; otherwise, how will people know it is heaven that we are representing?

One key passage of scripture gives us a challenging insight into how Jesus served to establish the reign of God. In his letter to the Christians at Philippi, Paul wrote what is sometimes considered to be the earliest hymn of the church, a wonderfully poetic and evocative statement of who Jesus is and how we should be like him: "Think of yourselves the way Christ Jesus thought of himself. He had equal status with God but didn't think so much of himself that he had to cling to the advantages of that status no matter what. Not at all. When the time came, he set aside the privileges of deity and took on the status of a slave, became human! Having become *human*, he stayed human. It was an incredibly humbling process. He didn't claim special privileges. Instead, he lived a selfless, obedient life and then died a selfless, obedient death—and the worst kind of death at that—a crucifixion" (Phil. 2:5-8, THE MESSAGE).

Paul was trying to get the church to look beyond a faith centered only on the church and focus instead on how they could live their lives for others. This passage gives insight into how we are to carry ourselves as Christians when participating in God's mission.

INCARNATION: GOD AMONG US

The focus of Paul's hymn is the Incarnation. God made flesh is a powerful statement about how much our world matters to God, its people, our situations, and our day-to-day realities. Our lives matter. Suffering, pain, and brokenness matter, so much so that God chooses to become part of it.

We engage in hands-on ministry on Christ's behalf so that God can be known in the world. We do not merely send money; we enter into situations of need and brokenness to show God's great love to others. The ministry of presence is powerful and often impacts the people we serve more deeply than any activity we might engage in while among them. One community said they had not felt God cared about them until a UMVIM team traveled from far away to show them God's love.[6]

We are mistaken if we think our presence brings God into a situation; God is already there. Our lives only give witness to the God who is already present and active in the world. God's presence can do wonders to those who feel God has abandoned them. UMVIM team members often remark on how their own faith is strengthened by those they serve. Their encounter with others allows them to meet God in a new way.

IN RELATIONSHIP WITH GOD AND GOD'S WORLD

We confidently assert that the essence of our witness is relationship because God chose to become a part of this world through Christ. God-with-us is God-among-us, God sharing every part of our lives. The ministry of Jesus reflected God's presence in the time he spent with people, especially those at the margins of society. The meals he shared, the conversations with outcasts and leaders alike, his concern for those who came to hear him speak, all remind us that the essence of our work is the forging of relationships.

Again, we are mistaken if we think it is our activities that are at the heart of mission. Constructing buildings, providing medical care, and helping with education projects are all important. But, more importantly, through these tasks we witness to the God among us.

GOD AS A SERVANT

God is with us and among us. God is also in fellowship with us. More than this is the fact that God sent Jesus to live among us as a servant, not always a popular concept or even comfortable language. Our world reacts negatively to the word *servant*, as countless people continue to be forced into the demeaning role of servanthood with their basic human rights denied them. Paul's words to the Philippians convey Jesus' incredible and willing surrender of status and privilege for the sake of others.

Jesus lived with the dispossessed, the weak, the outcast, and the ignored, showing us the way we are to serve. This is not to deny God's love for those in positions of power and influence. It does make clear, however, that the kingdom of God does not come through power or position; it comes through faithful, incarnational, relational engagement with those who need a gospel of hope and healing.

For over two thousand years, the church has been most effective when working from the edges of society. It has been most abusive and ineffective when it has restricted itself to working with, or acquiring, power and prestige.

Philippians 2:5-8 refers to Jesus as "emptying himself" ("setting aside the privileges of deity" in the version quoted above). Willful surrender is at the heart of Christian service. In most western cultures we often focus on our rights. While not denying that there are basic human rights that must be protected for the sake of the vulnerable across the globe, Christians throughout the centuries have surrendered their lives for the gospel. Sometimes this is as simple as giving up our "creature comforts" while we engage in some form of Christian mission; other times, it is more costly and demanding. Following Christ often puts us at odds with the world and may require us to carry our own cross.

SERVICE IN HUMILITY

Humility is another characteristic of Christ-centered living. Often our cultural ethos encourages us to strive to become leaders and gain attention. We train our children to achieve the highest goals possible. There is nothing wrong with this in and of itself, but sometimes it is difficult for us to be with others without trying to take charge or take over!

Our culture trains us to solve problems, to get the job done, to fix things. It is hard to enter quietly into situations and focus on relationships with this mind-set. With an appropriate understanding of cultural differences and a deepening respect for people of other cultures, however, we can be much more effective in our gospel work by letting go of the urge to take control.

Jesus grew up on the margins of society in a remote village in Galilee, a humble carpenter with no earthly power or possessions. He spent thirty years among his people before beginning his public ministry, a ministry he conducted with deep humility.

Living and serving with deep humility opens us to the realization that all mission is an exchange: we give but we also receive; we teach but we also learn; we seek to help others be transformed and we are transformed in the process. This mutuality in mission is at the heart of what it means to be a Christ follower.

An attitude of humility and mutuality also opens us up to pay careful attention to our context—to the lives, words, and actions of others. If we listen carefully we comprehend more, and we learn to enter meaningfully into the lives of those among whom God has placed us.

SEEKING GOD'S JUSTICE

The goal of our work on behalf of God's mission is to bring about a world that is once again attuned to God's will. This involves more than simply helping others with their immediate needs. It also calls us to deal with issues of justice as we explore the underlying causes of their needs. A United Methodist pastor put it like this: "The role of charity is to eliminate need. The role of justice is to eliminate the need for charity."[7]

Seeking justice is not easy, but it is a vital part of our work. It requires us to spend time understanding the context of our mission work, not just preparing for the tasks we might be undertaking or plan to undertake. Destructive behaviors continue to harm our planet and its people. Restoring our fallen world to God's great vision calls for the best expressions of human community.

Although the vision of our broken world made whole might not be realized in our lifetimes, it remains our goal. As we help communities by building homes, schools, and churches, as we help improve health care and community infrastructure, as we feed and clothe the poor and the needy, we work to transform society in accordance with the values Jesus demonstrated.

PURPOSE AND TASK

The goal of repairing our broken world is indeed a challenge and must shape our work. As we prepare ourselves to engage in this work, whether through Volunteers In Mission, an experience offered by our local church, or as our own personal commitment to God's mission we must remember that the *way* we do our work is as important as what we do.

Our work ought to reflect our ultimate purpose of sharing Christ's love. Reflecting on the nature of God's mission and the character of God's chosen instrument, Jesus, will help us to be more effective in mission and bear witness to God's coming kingdom.

EXPANDING CULTURAL AWARENESS

elmira Nazombe

The task of mission involves establishing and nurturing partnerships and relationships in order to act on behalf of God's purpose. The goal of mission is to deepen the sense of mutuality between different parts of a global faith community. The task of mission involves the encounter of different cultures, national histories, political systems and practices, levels of wealth and power, mission histories, faiths, and understandings of justice and how to achieve it. Each person in the encounter brings the intersection of these identities with him or her to the mission experience.

Understanding the elements and intersections that are present in the mission context plays a critical role for those involved in the mission experience. Everyone must work to understand three important concepts of the mission journey: Answering God's Call, Search Me and Know My Heart, and They Will Know We Are Christians by Our Love. These three concepts are not independent of one another but reinforce and overlap parts of the mission experience and the life of faith.

We can use the word *culture* as a shorthand way of talking about the aspects of identity listed above. We define culture as "the collection of fundamental beliefs people hold about how things should be and how one should behave. It's a way of looking at the values, attitudes, and beliefs shared by a common group of people. It is the mental programming that shapes our habits, beliefs, decision making, and the way we see the world. To put it more simply, culture is a set of beliefs, practices, and expressions that help to define the community's identity. The community's culture is expressed in part by its religious practices, clothing, food, art, politics, and play or social life."[8] This means culture is not just what we eat, how we dress, or the political system with which we align ourselves. Culture involves our attitudes, values, and activities we consider important.

Mission experiences challenge us to attempt to understand both our own culture and the cultures of others, testing our ability to be open to values, attitudes, and behaviors different from our own. Building an awareness of our own culture(s) is difficult because we learn our culture "unconsciously as children by transmission from one generation to another."[9] Understanding as much as we can about the cultures present in a mission context plays a critical role for those involved. For both host and volunteers, building this awareness will enhance and amplify the work that is to be accomplished and presents an important opportunity for enriching the learning experience and the possibilities for transformation.

In order to carry out the task of building mutuality in mission, both volunteers and members of the host community must work in different ways to accomplish the goal of mutuality. Hosts need to be welcoming of volunteers and willing to teach them not only about the specific mission task but, more importantly, about the host context. They need to share insights about their theological understanding and national histories and realities that will impact the mission task as they deepen their understanding together of what it means to answer God's call.

Volunteers should remember and perhaps even struggle with the roles they will play in the mission context. The first is that of guest and learner. The second is that of a member of the "family," although at times they may feel like a distant cousin or a long-absent brother or sister. "One in Christ" should not be misunderstood as instant familiarity or sameness. The exploration of the volunteer role will help volunteers understand the limitations of their actions in the host country. Visitors or distant relatives cannot act until they understand the situation in which they find themselves. They must carefully consider their actions in light of the need to be respectful of the understandings and realities of their hosts.

What national history and values will volunteers and hosts carry into the mission experience? How will these identities shape what each sees, hears, and understands?

Many of us will carry the culture of the United States with us on our mission journey. The racial, economic, ethnic, communal, and national experiences we have acquired from living in the United States informs our perspectives and attitudes. Factors such as these interact and shape our identity. Our identity is also shaped by our preferences, passions, and the ideas and objects we hold sacred.

Mission volunteers should recognize the fact that those we meet on our journeys share parallel experiences within their own cultures and will feel as strongly about their identities and perspectives as we do about our own. If a journey takes us outside our own country, the difference in perspectives and identities may be more obvious. If the journey takes us to communities different from our own, but still within the country from which we come, we must remain attentive to the possibility of different values and attitudes. One of the challenges of the mission journey is to live within a context where our values clash with those of others. It is essential that we learn to practice mutual respect.

This handbook employs three ways to talk about the exploration of the critical task of expanding our cultural awareness:

(1) Answering God's call—understanding the relationship between mission and culture through biblical reflection

(2) Searching and knowing our own hearts—understanding the identity, attitudes, and perspectives of others

(3) Learning to be known as Christians by our love—developing personal and collective actions that give witness to our affirmation of love and justice

ANSWERING GOD'S CALL

Hosts and volunteers can use the mission journey to look at the experiences of Jesus and the disciples on their own mission journeys, explore how cultural attitudes affected their ministry, and reflect on the similarities and differences between the biblical context and their own, sharing wisdom across cultures.

Biblical reflection is a meaningful way to think about the relationship between the understandings and attitudes discussed above and the mission task. Often, when we engage in Bible study we do not think about the cultural context in which the narrative occurs. When entering the mission experience, it is useful to take time to examine biblical passages through the lens of cultural awareness. It is also important to reflect on how the culture of the characters in the Bible affected their behavior, including that of Jesus and the disciples, particularly during their missionary travels.

Luke 13 is among the many texts in the New Testament that tells us about Jesus and his disciples on their mission journey. Often when they encountered someone in need, others criticized help they offered. It is important to remember that Jesus brought with him his own history and culture. He recognized the ailments of the woman. Perhaps she reminded him of someone he knew. The text suggests that her problem was not physical but spiritual or emotional.

As we consider our mission journey, we will need to consider the cultural, national, and religious rules we carry with us and those we may encounter. We may go to a country that has suffered economically and spiritually for a long time, "bent over" by poverty and hunger. We may see ourselves like Jesus bringing healing to those "bent over" by the harsh conditions and spiritual realities of their lives. As hosts, we may view volunteers as those coming from a place that is "bent over" by its own wealth and privilege. All of us, volunteers and hosts alike, should be aware of the cultural rules we may need to respect or challenge, and we also must be aware of how our own hypocrisies may be revealed. We have to be open to the opportunity of the transformation of our cultural and spiritual disabilities through our encounters with others.

Think of the mission experience: If you are a volunteer participating in a mission journey because you are answering a call for help, what attitudes might you bring with you and what attitudes might you encounter while you are there? If you are a host you are likely to be overjoyed to see the volunteers arrive and receive help, but you may also wonder what else they bring with them. Will volunteers be able to avoid feeling a sense of superiority because they are from a wealthy nation or community? As a host, do you worry that the volunteers will not respect your culture and that they may unknowingly break the rules?

Jesus, the bent over woman, the leader of the synagogue, perhaps even the crowd that witnesses it all—we can learn a great deal from imagining ourselves in the shoes of each person in the story.

SEARCH ME AND KNOW MY HEART

Working on our cultural awareness gives us a chance to look seriously at ourselves in order to understand others better and to work with them on God's mission. The mission journey provides a wonderful opportunity to listen, observe, learn, and grow with one another as we bring different histories and perspectives to the table, and, at the same time, share a common faith. The people we encounter can allow us to see ourselves in ways that we cannot apart from others. Hosts and volunteers must learn to respect each other's knowledge. This does not mean accepting as truth everything that is said or valued, but it does mean we are open to learning new truths and seeing the flaws in some of our beliefs.

Cultural awareness means digging deep to understand our own multiple identities and learning to listen to and understand the identities of others, as well as how these identities shape our perspectives of others.

Hosts have an opportunity to share not only vital information about the values and attitudes of their own country but also their experiences and attitudes about volunteers and volunteer countries. Mission volunteers should think deeply about their own identities. They should think about the aspects of daily life that are taken for granted but offer emotional comfort. This may reflect the relative affluence of the lives of many volunteers. Each volunteer should consider how he or she will respond if these things are not present in the mission context. What about electricity or easy access to the Internet? What about fast food or the ability to drive a car anywhere you want to go? These are cultural practices that are taken for granted, and volunteers must think about how they will react when these things are not present.

Another significant place of sharing can be the history and current state of mission relationships. This history can affect the mission experience. While it is a shared history, the perceptions of that history may vary. What is the current character of the relationships between those in the host community and your individual church, conference, or The United Methodist Church as a whole? Is it a relationship of independence and partnership, a relationship of dependency, or something in between? Hosts and volunteers alike carry that history with them, and they will see the results of that history in the host community. The financial, material, and program resources volunteers bring to the host community and the way in which they choose to share them can affect the relationships they hope to build.

KNOW WE ARE CHRISTIANS BY OUR LOVE

Both host and volunteer need to look deeper, to consider some of the key national values and attitudes that persons from their country carry with them—for example, fairness and generosity. What about the importance and value of the individual in terms of relationship to the community? How do these values manifest themselves in attitudes and behaviors within the mission context? What are our experiences with and attitudes toward people who are different from us, those from different races and economic classes, those who speak different languages? What is our comfort level with these differences? How will we handle living in a context where we are in the minority? How will this change our behavior?

Moreover, what are the patterns of justice and injustice that mark the attitudes of the host toward volunteers or volunteers toward the host? You may be seen as a representative of your government's policies and programs, policies and programs of which you may not be aware. What does it mean if these policies include military assistance to particular governments, media images of wealth, or practices of racial discrimination? Regardless of the volunteer's personal attitude or knowledge, hosts may see you as a representative of your government's policies and practices.

The joy and blessing of the mission journey is that it will generate new cultural perspectives created by the volunteers and the host community together.

VOLUNTEER MISSION EXPERIENCES AND SPIRITUAL TRANSFORMATION

Jane P. Ives

"See, I am doing a new thing! Now it springs up; do you not perceive it?"
Isaiah 43:19, NIV

A shy girl in her early teens traveled to Henderson Settlement in Frakes, Kentucky, for a two-week volunteer mission experience. She returned afire, ready to take on the world, and she began to serve as a leader in her church and community. Experienced mission volunteers know that such a response is not unusual. First timers, who may think they are simply responding to God's call to help others or going on an adventure, are often surprised to find how much they are changed. Members of the host community, perhaps hoping only to get a job done or a project completed, may be transformed as they encounter and develop relationships with the volunteers. Some persons may sign up for these experiences because they hunger for life-changing adventures, and veteran participants may keep going back because they welcome the transformation in themselves and want to continue to grow.

How can volunteers and hosts alike prepare ahead of time to fully experience such transformation? What can team leaders do during mission experiences to increase the likelihood that both volunteers and hosts will grow, rather than complete their time together unchanged or become overwhelmed and react negatively to the experience? How can leaders of volunteer and host teams follow up with participants afterward to ensure they do not dismiss these potentially life-changing events as interesting adventures or allow them to be pushed into the background by the pressures of daily life?

17

SPIRITUAL FORMATION AND TRANSFORMATION

Christians speak of spiritual formation as the process of becoming more Christlike, living in closer relationship to God, and being empowered by the Holy Spirit to live as God wants us to live. When spiritual formation brings about radical changes in our attitudes and behaviors, we call it transformation.

Paul, transformed by an encounter with Christ on the Damascus road, dramatically declares in his letter to the Roman church that "creation waits with eager longing for the revealing of the children of God, . . . in hope that the creation itself will be set free from its bondage to decay and will obtain the freedom of the glory of the children of God" (Rom. 8:19-21). He also challenges, "Do not be conformed to this world, but be transformed by the renewing of your minds, so that you may discern what is the will of God—what is good and acceptable and perfect" (Rom. 12:2). He reminds the Philippians that spiritual growth is not a result of our own striving, "for it is God who is at work in you, enabling you both to will and to work for his good pleasure" (Phil. 2:13). In Galatians he describes the outward signs of this process, "the fruit of the Spirit is love, joy, peace, patience, kindness, generosity, faithfulness, gentleness, and self-control" (Gal. 5:22-23).

Other faith communities may use different words to describe spiritual formation and transformation, but also seek to understand and live in accordance with the meaning and purpose of life as defined by their sacred texts and spiritual leaders. Most of us share a common belief in a mystery beyond outward appearances and daily events, a conviction of "something more," and a desire to understand and connect to that "Ultimate Reality" or "Higher Power." If mission experiences bring us together with persons of other faiths or persons not part of any organized religion, we know that Christ still calls us to love God and neighbor, whoever our neighbors may be. We might even learn something from them.

While we understand that God does the work of spiritual formation and transformation, we can actively open ourselves to this process and enhance it. Personal spiritual disciplines (prayer, Bible study, meditation, and fasting) and participation in communities of faith nurture and sustain us on our spiritual journeys. John Wesley called this "going on to perfection," holiness, and sanctification. More recently our church has begun to speak about making "disciples of Jesus Christ for the transformation of the world."[10] Toward that end, we offer a variety of experiences that can nurture spiritual formation and transformation.

HOW MISSION EXPERIENCES TRANSFORM US

United Methodist Volunteers In Mission (UMVIM) experiences offer a unique context for spiritual transformation. As Rueben Job comments in *A Guide to Retreat for All God's Shepherds,* we often become so immersed in our busy schedules and the noisy demands of our daily lives that we neglect to care for our souls.[11] The act of going to a different place and leaving our ordinary lives behind may open us to hear God speaking to us.

Unanticipated events in mission experiences, however, can trigger an even deeper level of transformation than may be possible during individual or group retreats. Volunteers sign up for mission experiences expecting to give and to experience the joy of helping others, but they are amazed when they find that they receive more than they give. Volunteers go thinking their faith is strong, but they find themselves humbled when they encounter persons of deep faith living in challenging situations. Seeing first-hand the difficult conditions in which others live and the suffering they endure because of natural disasters or human neglect and violence, they feel a rush of gratitude and realize their own privilege. When those who seem to have little wealth offer gracious and generous hospitality, volunteers feel ashamed, recognizing their own tendency toward selfishness and preoccupation with their possessions. They discover that they can cope with what they would never have chosen: uncomfortable living conditions and unfamiliar food. They learn to adjust expectations and stretch themselves to do what they never thought they could. They discover a common humanity with team members and with those they meet at the work site, and they learn to look beyond personal differences to see that all people are alike in that they want to love and be loved, to know that their lives matter, and to know that they have choices.[12]

Mission hosts may be surprised when preconceived ideas about volunteers prove to be untrue. They may harbor expectations shaped by stereotype and media images, as did a Russian woman who exclaimed in surprise that the American volunteers did not seem to be mean like the ones she had seen on television. Hosts may feel embarrassed by their poverty and the simplicity of their homes and possessions, and they may expect to be looked down on by their guests. Experiences with—or rumors about—volunteers who acted as if they were superior, made presumptuous requests, and complained incessantly may have disappointed and disillusioned their hosts. Hosts may try too hard to please, causing inconvenience and perhaps even hardship for themselves and their communities. Volunteers can overcome these negative expectations by treating their hosts as equals, by expressing appreciation for who they are and what they have to offer, and by demonstrating openness and willingness to learn. Mutual respect and consideration reflect a clear understanding of and appreciation for God's grace, abundantly available for all. God's grace makes true partnership possible.

NEW INSIGHTS

One of the startling aspects of mission volunteer experiences, especially for first-time participants, comes when they discover that God is already at work wherever they go. They may think—mistakenly—that we are bringing God as revealed to us in Jesus Christ to our destination. Our mission team members felt God's presence when we heard our Haitian host family's voices join in prayer before daylight, when we saw how they cared for one another and for us, and when we joined with them in long and fervent worship services. Encountering God and recognizing the power of the Holy Spirit already working for good in the lives of those we assist energizes us and inspires us to align ourselves with that power. Though we know that what we do is only a small part of the big picture, we feel assured that our contribution is vitally important.

Sometimes God speaks to us most clearly when we find ourselves in situations that are uncomfortable or even unbearable. Our partiality for sanitary conditions was challenged on a rural farm where flies invaded both our sleeping quarters and our eating space. Because we could do nothing to fix the situation we adjusted to it. We learned to sleep with our heads under our sheets to avoid our buzzing visitors and to wave our hands ceaselessly over our plates during meals. We survived, and we learned that we do not always have to have things our way. That insight can free volunteers to move outside their comfort zones with confidence that "[We] can do all things through Christ who strengthens [us]" (Phil. 4:13, NKJV).

We have to let go of the illusion of control when things do not occur on our timetable. Those of us who are impatient by nature or accustomed to having events unfold in a timely manner often struggle to stay positive and upbeat when we have to wait. Although careful planning is vital, we must learn not to get too attached to it. Because I sometimes single-mindedly attack my to-do list, a friend once said to me gently, "Let Jesus interrupt your agenda." During mission experiences, we may meet Jesus around every corner, presenting needs and challenges that we had not anticipated. We need to practice the spiritual disciplines of listening, observing what is happening around us, and paying attention to what God is calling us to do.

Likewise, living in close proximity with other members of our mission team compels us to build good working relationships with others, sometimes with persons we might not otherwise choose as friends. Hopefully we learn to accept and deal with differences and to resolve conflicts in ways that meet the various needs of all involved. We can learn to speak our feelings and needs without attacking or blaming others, and to listen actively with curiosity and open minds, trying to truly understand the other's point of view. We might discover that our way is not the only way and that how we see the world is no better than the point of view of another, nor is it necessarily right. Paul writes, "By the grace given me I say to every one of you: Do not think of yourself more highly than you ought, but rather think of yourself with sober judgment, in accordance with the measure of faith God has given you" (Rom. 12:3, NIV).

Worship during mission experiences usually includes both intimate team gatherings and more formal services for the visitors and hosts, planned and led by either or both groups. We may find ourselves worshiping in a language we do not understand, as well as participating in rituals and traditions foreign to us. Worship in some cultures may seem so dramatic and emotional that we feel uncomfortable or wish that our worship back home could be more exciting. We may be amazed to feel the Holy Spirit moving in us even when we do not know the words or understand the litany. Worshiping together strengthens the bond between visitors and hosts and builds mutual respect and trust.

CULTIVATING SPIRITUAL TRANSFORMATION

A botany professor explained "cultivation" to me as the process of opening up soil to allow oxygen, water, and nutrients to penetrate and move through it. Mission experiences stir things up for visiting volunteers and hosts alike. When persons in an increased state of openness spend time studying and reflecting on scripture, it will more likely take root in them and bear fruit. By asking good questions and allowing time for thoughtful responses (both individual journaling and group discussion), leaders can help participants deepen their understanding and consider applications to their own lives. The reflection process is essential because participants will more likely recall and integrate into their lives what they conclude for themselves (see "Engaging in Group Conversation," pages 49–51).

"But as for what was sown on good soil, this is the one who hears the word and understands it, who indeed bears fruit and yields, in one case a hundredfold, in another sixty, and in another thirty" (Matt. 13:23).

Some volunteer and host leaders have found it beneficial to appoint a specific person to act as a spiritual guide for their team. The spiritual guide works with the team leader, assisting with orientation, helping members know one another, and assuming responsibility for devotional times, Bible study, and other spiritual practices, including use of the meditations provided for BEFORE, DURING, and AFTER a mission experience. The spiritual guide and team leader can also work together to help team members process their experiences, respond to team dynamics, and deal effectively with individual needs and interpersonal conflicts should they arise. The spiritual guides of both teams can work together to coordinate assignments for table grace, devotional leadership, team rituals, and shared worship times, giving those who would like to lead the opportunity to do so.

The following sections of this handbook provide guidelines, tools, and activities for cultivating spiritual transformation and sensitivity to cultural differences and justice issues BEFORE, DURING, and AFTER a mission experience.

Dear friends, now we are children of God, and what we will be has not yet been made known. But we know that when [Christ] appears, we shall be like him, for we shall see him as he is (1 John 3:2, NIV).

CHRISTIAN MISSION IN A TIME OF GLOBALIZATION
DOING JUSTICE OUTSIDE THE GATE!

David Wildman

Establish justice in the gate.
—Amos 5:15

The term *globalization* describes the increasingly rapid, massive, and international movements of money, people, goods, and information throughout the world in recent years. Globalization involves processes of transnational economic and cultural integration that make us all more interconnected and interdependent than ever before. It also involves growing divides—gates—between the powerful few and the impoverished and excluded many. How do we go about God's mission in a world such as this?

> *Globalization involves growing divides—gates—between the powerful few and the impoverished and excluded many.*

Today, the Internet and social media symbolize the exponential growth in global communication and flow of information. At the same time, the notion of a "digital divide" reminds us that access to this wealth of information and technology is profoundly limited.

For much of the nineteenth and twentieth centuries, the nation state was the primary frame of reference for organizing political and economic relations (as well as many church denominations). Even mission was divided into "foreign mission" and "home mission." In today's context of globalization, the corporation has largely replaced the nation-state as a model for institutional organization. Fortune 500 companies now have larger operating budgets than the gross domestic product of most developing nations. Of the one hundred largest economies in the world today, fifty-two are corporations and forty-eight are nation-states. As economies become increasingly globalized, the corporation serves more as an implicit reference point for structuring institutions, relations throughout society, and even our sense of mission. Churches often speak of "global mission." Global Ministries now defines our mission as "from anywhere to anywhere." This description recognizes both the transnational reality of United Methodists as well as the growing dominance of corporate structures in shaping our institutions.

International financial institutions such as the World Trade Organization, the World Bank, and the International Monetary Fund have taken on the mission of gatekeeping, regulating and enforcing the rules concerning the flow of resources across the globe. The benefits of globalization, however, do not flow equally between those inside and those outside the gate. A critical part of mission work involves examining the many gates and gatekeepers in today's global economy that create and sustain unjust relations.

In the Bible, the gate represents a significant place where communities gather, where the marketplace is located, and where those inside and those outside the gate meet to trade and resolve disputes. In using the image of the gate and the division between communities inside and outside, it is crucial to stress that there are equally important and divisive gates inside each nation as there are between rich and impoverished nations. Trade agreements, in effect, establish economic and military gates and gatekeepers that regulate trade and movement of goods, resources, and people between those inside the gate and those outside it, primarily for the benefit of those on the inside.

HOW GLOBALIZATION AFFECTS TODAY'S SENSE OF MISSION

1. Standardization/Containerization. One of the key technological developments of globalization has been the use of standardized containers in shipping goods. Containers, with the help of a computerized tracking system, can move interchangeably and easily from trucks to trains to ships with minimal labor. This greatly expands the speed and ease of transport of goods. Much of our culture is containerized and prepackaged to ease shipping to more places.

Containers also serve as places where impoverished and desperate immigrants hide in the hope of safe passage to nations where the resources are shipped. Thousands of airtight containers filled with war material and aid are shipped to Afghanistan. After decades of war, there is little need for the containers to export products back to other places. Afghans now use containers as ready-made shops and community health clinics.

In the abundance of your trade you were filled with violence (Ezekiel 28:16).

Standardization has brought about expansion in efficiency and quantity of outcome, but what impact has it had on the quality of our missional relations? Ezekiel warned of the violence connected with the rapid expansion of trade in a place like Tyre. As we seek stronger connections in mission, it is critical to reflect on some of the ways we are already connected, like Tyre, through trade with many faraway places.

> Read Ezekiel chapters 26-28 and reflect on how they continue to speak about just and unjust global relations today.

2. Decentralization of Production/Concentration of Wealth. Take a moment to examine the labels of clothes and other products you use. Most of us are a walking United Nations in what we wear and use each day. Now reflect on the source of food you eat. How much was grown locally? How much of it comes from places far away?

While more goods are circulating across the globe, the profits from this rapid global economic expansion are becoming increasingly concentrated in the hands of a few individuals. The disparity in income between transnational CEOs and the workers who make the products has never been wider. At the same time there is a growing concentration in decision making as corporations displace governments in certain areas. The model for democracy and community decision making is now based more on one share, one vote than on one person, one vote.

> On a map, put dots to identify how interconnected we are in the resources we depend on each day. Do we know the people who made these products? Have we visited their communities? What do we know about the conditions under which they work?

25

> How do we make decisions in our mission work? Who is included? Who is missing from the table? Should those with the most financial resources have the most say?

3. Privatization of Profit and Socialization of Risks and Costs. While many people praise the private sector over public sector programs, everything is not privatized under globalization. The environmental and social risks of business failure are seen as social responsibilities that all citizens must bear. Cigarette companies, arms manufacturers, toxic chemical corporations, and oil and coal companies all have as their primary mission to glean private profits from wherever they can. The devastating consequences of their expanding mission is a matter that society is forced to bear.

Moreover, public goods such as water, sanitation, electrical power, and public lands are under pressure in many places to be privatized for profit, which means many people will be left outside the gate without access to these goods or the ability to participate in building up the common good. Governments have encouraged the privatization of services, and they have asked churches and other humanitarian organizations to voluntarily alleviate the sufferings created by the negative forces of globalization. Mission as justice work means asking about hidden costs and consequences that may devastate the lives of our sisters and brothers.

4. Access as a Key Issue for Mission in a Context of Globalization. Just because a product is available in an increasing number of markets does not mean more people can enjoy its use. Over one billion people lack access to safe drinking water and adequate sanitation. Almost half the world's population lives on less than two dollars a day. What can two dollars a day buy? People working in low-paying service jobs inside the gate can only afford a place to live that is outside the gate. Still, many impoverished nations of the global south, such as the Philippines, depend on remittances from migrant workers working in rich countries inside the gate to support local families and economies back home.

Mission as justice work means asking about hidden costs and consequences that may devastate the lives of our sisters and brothers.

5. Public/Private Partnerships. Goodwill and voluntary arrangements between unequal partners are often posed as a solution to the problems of globalization. The commitment to the common good and to public (shared) responsibility is increasingly privatized. In an ecumenical meeting with the South African Council of Churches, participants affirmed that any partnership in a context of unequal power relations is nothing more than domination. In many North American suburban communities, landscape crews of migrant workers have traveled great distances to help wealthy families. They send stories about their experiences back home. Take a moment to reflect on the similarities and differences between an UMVIM experience doing manual labor and the experience of migrant workers doing similar types of work.

THE CHALLENGE OF MISSION IN AN UNJUST WORLD

Today's global economic system embodies a process of controlling, grabbing, and extracting more and more resources. Like colonization, this continues a process that uproots, displaces, and separates peoples from their lands and from one another for the benefit of a few.

Ezekiel wrote during a period of colonization and displacement related to the unjust and violent trade practices of Tyre. Three chapters of the book are devoted to condemning the injustices occurring in Tyre (26–28). Ezekiel offers God's alternative concepts of justice based on meeting people's needs: "[God says] I will bind up the injured, and I will strengthen the weak, but the fat and strong I will destroy. I will feed them with justice. . . . I will make with them a covenant of peace and banish wild animals from the land, so that they may live in the wild and sleep in the woods securely" (Ezek. 34:16, 25).

The disparity in control over trade and misuse of resources exposes the heart of the crisis Ezekiel repeatedly portrays. For Ezekiel, restoring people's security and relationship with the land is the basis for just economic relations, not the other way around. Yet powerful gatekeepers in today's global economy continually divide people against one another (for example, immigrant workers against citizen workers) so that the many labor to heap up profits for the few.

Mission that is free trade oriented often portrays us all as shoppers, the world as a marketplace, and mission encounters as if everyone in the marketplace is equal. This ignores the historical origins of economic injustice. The narrative found in Genesis 41–47 about Joseph and the famine depicts a contrast between a plan of sharing scarce resources for the common good and how scarcity combined with government policies gradually strips subsistence farming communities of their resources and their land. When Joseph interprets Pharaoh's dream, he outlines a mission plan of devoting 20 percent of the harvest toward the common good for future times of hardship (Gen. 41:33-36). In the implementation of Joseph's plan, those who labor are gradually forced to spend all their money, sell their livestock, sell their land and labor, and give a portion of the wealth to Pharaoh (Gen. 47:13-26).

When small farmers today lose their land, they find it impossible to participate on an equal footing with large landowners, corporations, or well-meaning, well-resourced mission teams. Forced off their land, they must hit the road and migrate to survive. They become vulnerable to further forms of exploitation when traveling along dangerous highways and byways outside the gates. Landless migrants are especially vulnerable to exploitative slave-labor conditions in sweatshops and inner cities. By contrast, the Bible repeatedly tells stories of God's mission leveling the powerful and uplifting the oppressed as the only way to restore a covenant of justice and peace in our global relations.

MARKET FUNDAMENTALISM: A DEVOURING MODEL

The Bible tells history from the underside—from the perspective of poor farmers, migrant workers, the landless, widows, orphans, and the oppressed. When the prophets and Jesus confront the powerful, they often use metaphorical language common to the daily lives of the people. It makes sense that Nahum would depict unjust merchants as locusts. The economic injustice of traders, government officials, and the rich are compared to the predatory, devouring dangers of wild animals.

You have increased the number of your merchants till they are more than the stars in the sky, but like locusts they strip the land and then fly away (Nah. 3:16, NIV).

Malachi makes a similar allusion to the devouring ways of economic injustice: "Then I will draw near to you for judgment . . . against those who oppress the hired workers in their wages, the widow and the orphan, against those who thrust aside the alien. . . . I will rebuke the locust for you, so that it will not destroy the produce of your soil; and your vine in the field shall not be barren" (Mal. 3:5, 11).

From European colonialism to neo-liberal, free trade globalization today, the dominant development model exerts dominion over all creation. It treats the natural world as an immense treasure chest of goods to be owned, extracted, exploited, traded, devoured, and discarded by those who have the power to do so. The well-being of humans is measured primarily in quantitative terms and depends on competing in and winning the global trade game. Proponents of this model contend that the poor do not work hard enough and should be left to the church's mission.

For many European and North American missionaries in the past, the mission of Christianity is intimately linked with the spread of Western commerce and civilization. In 1857, the British missionary-explorer and colonialist David Livingstone saw the church's mission as intertwined with a Western sense of trade and civilization. Livingstone says, "For the purposes of commerce [and] as civilization and Christianity must go on together, I was obliged to find a path to the sea, in order that I should not sink to the level of the natives." Where is the mutuality in this approach to mission?[13]

Listen, you heads of Jacob and rulers of the house of Israel! Should you not know justice—you who hate the good and love the evil, who tear the skin off my people, and the flesh off their bones. . . . Your wealthy are full of violence (Mic. 3:1-2; 6:12).

A triangular alliance among merchants, missionaries, and marine soldiers served colonial powers and corporate interests at the expense of the colonized communities. For years, the biblical imagery of light versus dark was exploited by white Christians to justify a predatory, life-destroying economic system of slavery, enabling a few individuals to accumulate vast fortunes. Supporters of free trade have long insisted that the more nations and people participating in the global market and the more goods that are traded, the better off we will be. Developing nations were urged to go into debt to expand their export trade capacity.

Some churches act as if free trade and corporate rights are a gospel truth guiding our sense of mission. A perspective such as this equates defending free trade and corporate interests by any means necessary with defending faith and the civilized world, and vice versa. By contrast, Jesus reminds us, "No one can serve two masters. . . . You cannot serve God and wealth" (Matt. 6:24). The current global market economy and a market-oriented approach to mission are neither sustainable nor just for the vast majority of people.

MISSION OUTSIDE THE GATE

In Jesus' day, the Roman Empire built a vast system of interconnected roads, viaducts, and shipping ports. These served primarily to speed up the transport of goods and soldiers from one part of the empire to another. Roads connected one walled city with another to limit exposure to the dangers outside the gate. Roman roads were a globalizing force that increased trade, communication, and control over a widespread area. These same roads were crucial for the spread of the gospel in the early church. Church mission became globalized beyond Palestine by the same trade routes that the Roman armies traveled. It was frequently outside the gate on these dangerous roads where Christians were most active in mission. Paul and Silas met Lydia outside the gate. It is also where Paul cured the girl who was a slave, challenging the profit-making interests of those inside the gate (Acts 16).

"A man was going down from Jerusalem to Jericho, when he fell into the hands of robbers" (Luke 10:30).

Churches from the early 1900s until today continue to stand with all who find themselves at the gates of our globalized society: with workers at factory gates and "free-enterprise zone" gates who work in sweatshops and earn barely enough to survive; at ports with seafarers who move goods for others but have few rights of their own; with migrant workers at national borders between developed nations and developing nations who are judged guilty by the location of their birth; with landless farm workers whose lands have been taken and who now must work for others.

Paul reminds us that meeting basic needs and sustaining one another's communities is what it means to be members of the same body with gifts "for the common good" (1 Cor. 12:7). The sustainable ordering of society will require participation by all "in order that there may be a fair balance" (2 Cor. 8:14). This requires churches within the United States to examine their lifestyles, consumption, and wasteful practices as part of being in mission and partnership with impoverished neighbors near and far.

Churches face a crucial choice regarding global trade, global poverty, and global mission: whose side are we on and what drives our mission? Will concern about return on the shares in middle-class church endowments and individual pension funds lead us to align our mission with corporate interests more than the well-being of others? Or will we base our mission on justice and participation by all God's children, particularly by the marginalized and migrant peoples? Nearly fifty years ago, Dr. Martin Luther King Jr. posed the challenge we still face today: "When machines and computers, profit motives and property rights are considered more important than people, the giant triplets of racism, materialism, and militarism are incapable of being conquered."[14]

We went outside the gate by the river, where we supposed there was a place of prayer; and we sat down and spoke to the women who had gathered there (Acts 16:13).

In the same speech Dr. King goes on to call for a revolution of values: "A true revolution of values will soon cause us to question the fairness and justice of many of our past and present policies. On the one hand we are called to play the good Samaritan on life's roadside; but that will be only an initial act. One day we must come to see that the whole Jericho road must be transformed so that men and women will not be constantly beaten and robbed as they make their journey on life's highway. True compassion is more than flinging a coin to a beggar; it is not haphazard and superficial. It comes to see that an edifice which produces beggars needs restructuring."[15]

Our connectional heritage as United Methodists insists that the negative forces of globalization, racism, and militarism are not the way. God invites us to join in the mission of transforming the Jericho roads outside the gates in our own time. Mission as solidarity and a deeper connectedness with sisters and brothers who are marginalized and excluded promises new and abundant life for us all.

Paul reminds us that gate-crashing communities in mission with one another are awkward, motley road construction crews that embody what it means to be members of the same body with gifts "for the common good" (1 Cor. 12:7). A sustainable ordering of society requires participation by all "in order that there may be a fair balance" (2 Cor. 8:14).

MISSION AS ACCOMPANIMENT

As we seek to accompany one another in the mission of transforming dangerous, unjust roads into ways of justice, let us take to heart a central mission goal of Global Ministries: "We will participate with people oppressed by unjust economic, political, and social systems in programs that seek to build just, free and peaceful societies." Mission in partnership with communities oppressed by unjust systems is not a onetime event but a journey God keeps inviting us to take together.

Accompaniment reminds us of the relational nature of our faith and the relational nature of mission. Accompaniment means significant time devoted to walking with one another and sharing meals, joys, and pains together. It also involves surfacing conflicts and inequities that threaten to keep us divided. We often fail to recognize that mission in a community is not the same as accompanying one another in the work of justice.

Many stories in the Bible consider the idea of mission as accompaniment. Two stories frequently lifted up are Ruth and Naomi (Ruth 1) and the Emmaus road experience (Luke 24:13-35). Ruth and Naomi are widows who face an impoverished, uncertain future. Ruth's declaration to Naomi epitomizes the heart of accompaniment that crosses borders and cultures: "Where you go I will go, and where you stay I will stay. Your people will be my people and your God my God" (Ruth 1:16, NIV). Ruth becomes a migrant farm worker in a foreign land vulnerable to exploitation and sexual harassment as she faithfully accompanies Naomi. What can we learn from today's migrant workers about accompaniment and mission?

We often fail to recognize that mission in a community is not the same as accompanying one another in the work of justice.

The church has long turned to the Emmaus story as a lesson in discipleship, but this story also offers key insights on mission as accompaniment. Cleopas and his friend dare to share their hopes for liberation from unjust Roman rule with a stranger: "We had hoped that he was the one who was going to redeem Israel" (Luke 24:21, NIV). In the context of Jesus' recent public execution and a climate of fear and repression, this bold act of reaching out begins to forge a deeper connection with God's mission. As Cleopas and his companion travel farther from the dangers of Jerusalem and head closer to the safety of home, they still do not get it. Only when they extend hospitality to a stranger are their eyes opened. They now feel compelled to risk the dangers of the road at night and return to the teeth of Roman military might for the sake of a community still frozen by fear.

Mission as accompaniment involves stepping beyond our comfort zones and giving ourselves to the idea of love of God and love of neighbor. Today, Christian Peacemaker Teams (CPTs) and the World Council of Churches Ecumenical Accompaniment Program in Palestine and Israel (EAPPI) exemplify Christians accompanying communities facing violence and repression. What can we learn about accompaniment and mission from communities subjected to political repression, systemic discrimination, and armed violence? When have we stepped out of our comfort zones to join with others in transforming unjust systems?

We should not pretend that accompaniment in God's mission for justice is ever easy. Unlike natural disasters, injustice involves harmful, dehumanizing actions by people that devastate the lives of others. Moreover, victims of injustice are often blamed for their own suffering. Many of the gates and gatekeepers in our globalized world serve to create barriers between communities and render persons into spectators in the face of injustice and violence. Take a moment to reflect on some of the unjust systems and practices that divide us today. What steps would enable us to move from spectators of injustice to accompaniers for justice?

TRANSFORMING RELATIONS THROUGH ACCOMPANIMENT

The prophet Isaiah depicts one of the most powerful yet unlikely images of accompaniment in the Bible—the peaceable kingdom. In Isaiah 11:1-9 and 65:17-25, the wolf and lamb live together and the lion eats straw like the ox. Such accompaniment was as implausible in Isaiah's day as it is in our own. The image remains a powerful one, however, where predatory violence, insecurity, and fear are replaced by cooperation and harmony in a new, just community.

"The wolf and the lamb shall feed together" (Isaiah 65:25).

Try to imagine how this accompaniment begins. Did the lamb say to the wolf, "There are many predators out there, would you accompany me so that we can both be safe together?" Or perhaps the wolf said to the lamb, "Would you join me for lunch?" Ironically, the powerful wolf depends on the weak lamb in order to survive while the lamb does not trust or need the wolf. The wolf is a constant death-dealing threat. How do we transform predatory relationships into ones based on mutual respect and trust?

The image of wolves and sheep is often used to reflect the unequal, threatening power dynamics in human relations. A wolf in sheep's clothing is one example. Another example is, "Democracy is two wolves and one lamb voting on what to have for lunch; liberty is a well-armed lamb." This goes against the vision of transformative mission embodied in Isaiah and the Gospels. Matching a predator's threat with a counterthreat simply escalates the capacity for violence and keeps everyone hostage to fear. By contrast, Jesus describes mission this way: "See, I am sending you out like sheep into the midst of wolves; so be wise as serpents and innocent as doves" (Matt. 10:16).

Isaiah depicts peaceful accompaniment of the wolf and lamb together and closely connected with God's mission for economic justice. In Isaiah 11 the prophet envisions new leadership that "will not judge by what he sees with his eyes, . . . but with righteousness he will judge the needy, with justice he will give decisions for the poor of the earth" (vv. 3-4, NIV). In chapter 65 predatory economic practices will cease and day laborers and farmworkers will receive the fruits of their labors: "No longer will they build houses and others live in them, or plant and others eat. . . . They will not labor in vain, nor will they bear children doomed to misfortune" (vv. 22-23, NIV).

Isaiah and the other prophets also use wolves and lions to condemn the exploitative practices of the powerful that prey on and impoverish so many of their neighbors. In one of his harshest critiques, the prophet Ezekiel proclaims, "Its princes within it are like a roaring lion tearing the prey; they have devoured human lives; they have taken treasure and precious things; they have made many widows within it. . . . Its officials within it are like wolves tearing the prey, shedding blood, destroying lives to get dishonest gain" (Ezek. 22:25, 27). We participate in transformative mission for justice when we work to end predatory practices without destroying or demonizing the wolves.

> Share mission stories about wolves, sheep, serpents, and doves that each of us has encountered. What can we learn from one another about accompanying each other in the mission of justice?

BALAAM'S DONKEY AND THE CHALLENGES OF ACCOMPANIMENT

The story of Balaam and his donkey is about the challenges we face in accompaniment. Balaam has an urgent, prophetic mission, and he focuses on accomplishing it. The donkey, on the other hand, recognizes imminent danger and strives to protect herself and Balaam, her partner in mission. Despite repeated beatings, she remains faithful and creative in finding alternative paths to safety for them both. Oppressed communities, like Balaam's lowly donkey, often find themselves saddled with well-trained, mission-minded visitors who ignore their grassroots wisdom. The story of Balaam's donkey challenges a dominant view from above, both in biblical times and today, that takes poor communities for granted as little more than beasts of burden fit for serving the well-informed and well-resourced.

*"Why have you beaten your donkey these three times?
I have come here to oppose you because your path is a
reckless one before me"* (Num. 22:32, NIV).

The story concludes with Balaam acknowledging how blind he was to God's wisdom and his desire to reconnect with God's mission. Instead of fearing more failure, Balaam learns from his mistakes and humbly steps out again into mission.

> *Let us then go to [Jesus] outside the camp and bear the abuse he endured* (Hebrews 13:13).

The wisdom of the world is turned on its head when we affirm the fact that the views from below—of a donkey, perhaps—open our eyes to the divine presence in mission. Even a donkey can be wiser than the wisest of the privileged. Isaiah opens by comparing the wisdom of a donkey with the folly of a nation and its leaders: "The ox knows his master, the donkey its owner's manger, but Israel does not know, my people do not understand" (Isa. 1:3, NIV). Paul also challenges the church in Corinth to rethink its approach to mission: "But God chose what is foolish in the world to shame the wise; God chose what is weak in the world to shame the strong; God chose what is low and despised in the world, things that are not, to reduce to nothing things that are, so that no one might boast in the presence of God" (1 Cor. 1:27-29).

> Reflect on how the perspectives of Balaam and the donkey, as well as Isaiah and First Corinthians, invite us all to rethink mission as accompaniment in our justice work.

ERODING INJUSTICE

In a context of widespread violence and economic injustice, Jesus tells a story about our "need to pray always and not to lose heart" (see Luke 18:1-8). The story is about the confrontation between a poor widow and an unjust judge.

The text does not say how the widow's husband died. Perhaps he was a sharecropper working sixteen or twenty hours a day to pay off his debts and died of a heart attack. Perhaps he died in an accident while fishing or working as a bricklayer. Perhaps he was robbed on his way home. Or maybe he was imprisoned for his inability to pay his debts and died there. Perhaps he was pressed into the Roman army and died far away. Or maybe in the Roman war against the Zealots he was what today would be called "collateral damage." Maybe he was a Zealot himself. We do not know. But certainly there were many women in the communities to whom Jesus told this story who were widows.

The Bible contains many stories on the importance of providing for widows and orphans. In this story, the widow, one of the most vulnerable members of society, is not an object of charity but a model of leadership in mission for justice. The story challenges all who hear it to take on her tenacity in our common mission towards justice.

"Because this widow keeps bothering me, I will grant her justice, so that she may not wear me out by continually coming"
(Luke 18:5).

The first lesson we glean from the widow's story is that mission is not primarily about charity. Mission involves joining with the poor in working for justice and eradicating poverty. While the burden of poverty falls heaviest on women and children, such vulnerability does not mean a lack of capacity. The widow did not wait for help from someone else; she voiced her own complaint. Jesus repeatedly lifts up the downtrodden as models of faithfulness and leaders in the mission of justice.

A second lesson we take away from the story of the widow is that while the unjust judge never converts, he does change his behavior. How often have we hoped that if only those in power would see what we have seen or hear what we have heard they would change their minds and policies? The widow's struggle for justice embodies a mission of erosion; she slowly wears down the resistance of the powerful through her persistence. She keeps at it, and she inspires us to do the same.

The prophet Amos proclaims, "Let justice roll down like waters, and righteousness like an ever-flowing stream" (Amos 5:24). Like a stream slowly carving a canyon, justice through mission requires steady movement to erode the banks of resistance. The Montgomery Bus Boycott in Montgomery, Alabama, began with one woman, Rosa Parks, but took the steady, persistent efforts of a whole community to erode segregation. Farm worker boycotts employ years of mounting pressure to get companies to pay better wages and improve conditions in the fields. The persistent widow, through the steady flow of her entreaties, wore down the resistance of a powerful official in an unjust system.

A third lesson we can glean from the widow is the fact that she voices her demands for justice publicly. During the time in which this story occurs, judges were village elders who heard cases in a public place—the city gate. The market, located at the gate, was where farmers who worked the land outside the gate would sell to wealthy people who lived inside the gate. We do not know the nature of the widow's case, but we do know that the widow boldly and persistently demands justice at the gate.

For Amos, the gate was a place to make unjust authorities uncomfortable and call them to account: "They hate the one who reproves in the gate, and they abhor the one who speaks the truth. . . . For I know how many are your transgressions, . . . you who afflict the righteous, who take a bribe, and push aside the needy in the gate" (Amos 5:10, 12).

Maybe a prominent landlord did not allow the widow to glean his fields as required in the law. Maybe her home was foreclosed by one of the wealthy scribes about whom Jesus warns, "Beware of the scribes. . . they devour widow's houses" (Luke 20:45-47). Whatever the case, her public confrontation with the judge undoubtedly stirred the crowd into joining her in pressing the judge to act justly. Like Amos, the widow keeps speaking truth to power and inviting those around her to stop being victims or spectators and join together in a mission of erosion. Her tireless truth-telling led to the transformation that Amos calls for: "Hate evil and love good, and establish justice in the gate" (Amos 5:15).

When we join in mission with the oppressed and impoverished, we become, drop by drop, like a cleansing rain that erodes the unjust systems that create too many beggars and widows in our own day.

PHASE
TWO

**EXPANDING CULTURAL AWARENESS
AND CULTIVATING SPIRITUAL
TRANSFORMATION**

INTRODUCTION

Many of us who have been involved in UMVIM experiences realize that while "Faith without works is dead" (Jas. 2:20), missional works without attention to spiritual formation are lifeless as well. It is easy to become infatuated with the work of mission and to participate without doing the spiritual work of discipling or becoming more Christlike. Team leaders, if they are not already aware, learn quickly that without intentional spiritual nurturing, mission volunteers soon experience burnout and may actually harm themselves and others. Michael Stewart, founding director of the Verge Network, compares mission without discipling to a car without an engine. No matter how shiny and impressive the car, without an engine it will go nowhere.[1]

The purpose of this handbook is to lift up the discipling aspects of mission experiences and to help team leaders—volunteer or host—guide participants through their time together in such a way that the transformation of their lives is maximized. Spiritual transformation includes a deepened commitment to bridge cultural differences and to correct the injustices rampant in our world. Team leaders have the opportunity not only to lead successful mission experiences but also to join in God's transforming work in the world.

Phase Two of this handbook is organized into three time frames or components of the mission experience:

> BEFORE—Planning, preparing, and leading at least three orientation sessions for team members
> DURING—Everything done with the team while actually engaged in the mission experience
> AFTER—Following up with team members to help them process the experience, interpret it to others, and incorporate new insights and understandings into their lives

Before these three sections is a Bible study to use the first time you gather as a team, a document describing strategies for engaging participants in group conversations, and a handout on spiritual centering that you may duplicate and distribute to your team members.

The material in this handbook is also organized around three themes that permeate any mission experience and addresses the task of discipling. Mission experiences usually begin when we answer a "call," either directly from God or in response to a specific need or request from persons seeking assistance. When we answer our call, we should seek God's guidance as we engage in searching ourselves and consider the extent to which we are equipped to serve and contribute positively to the experience. We must recognize both the strengths we bring to the experience and the areas in which we need to grow, knowing that the mission experience may test us in ways we have not been tested before. We build relationships both with our teammates and with those we encounter at the mission site while engaged in the mission experience. As we grow in our understanding of what it means to love and as we discover the unjust realities of our world, we deepen our commitment to Christ and resolve to follow him more faithfully.

Whether this is your first time as an UMVIM team leader or host, or you have led or hosted many other mission experiences, we hope this will enrich your experience and equip you more fully for the challenges and opportunities ahead.

LIVING OUR FAITH IN MISSION: A STUDY ON LUKE 10

Jeremy Basset

In Phase One, we outlined a theology of Christian mission. The purpose of this section was to promote actions on behalf of God's mission that are consistent with what we know about Jesus.

Phase Two applies the theological foundation developed in Phase One to the way we reflect on issues of culture, justice, and spiritual formation. What follows is intended to encourage personal and/or group reflection on the "Jesus attitude" to sharing the gospel with others.

The format of Phase Two invites readers to attend to issues that arise BEFORE, DURING, and AFTER the mission journey.

This Bible study sets the scene for what follows in the rest of the handbook, expanding on the principles outlined in Phase One, and offers guidance on the practical application of those principles.

If you are engaging in this study with others, reflect on the questions before having any group discussion. It is more important that you engage and discuss the passage from your own perspective and allow your own ideas or those of the group to stimulate your thinking before looking at the notes at the end of the section.

Remember, this study is for the first time you gather as a team. It will help focus your team on the bigger picture of mission as outlined in Phase One.

JESUS SENDS OUT THE SEVENTY

Luke 10:1-9, 17-21

BEFORE

Verses 1-4: The Job Description

1. What does it mean that Jesus sent seventy "others" (rather than the twelve disciples) on this mission and that he did it so early in his ministry?

2. Jesus does not disguise the challenges of mission. What do you see these challenges to be, and how are we meant to cope in the face of them?

3. What are some of the "wolves" that Christians face today in their participation in God's mission?

4. Why did Jesus tell the seventy not to take any resources with them? In what way is this relevant to our work today?

DURING

Verses 5-9: The Mission Context

5. What is our mission task if, as this passage seems to indicate, the context of our mission is being in relationship with a community and not any specific task or event?

6. Eating together seems to be an important aspect of this mission. What does this imply for us in our activity?

7. What does it mean that Jesus spent so much time eating with others and that he focused his ministry on a meal that we now call The Lord's Supper?

8. How are these disciples to convey the gospel in their work?

AFTER

Verses 17-21: Connected to Jesus

9. While the seventy are excited at what they can do, Jesus wants them to rejoice in something else. What does Jesus want them to rejoice in and why is it important?

10. In response to the seventy's experience in mission, Jesus is filled with the joy of the Holy Spirit. What does this mean and why is it important for us to know this about Jesus?

11. What advantage do the childlike have in participating in God's mission over those who think themselves wise and clever?

12. What might the next steps have been for these missionaries? How is this relevant for our participation in God's mission today?

NOTES ON LIVING OUR FAITH IN MISSION: A STUDY ON LUKE 10

1. These "rookies" knew little about Jesus at this stage, yet they were prepared to go as he asked. Remember, this occurs before Jesus' crucifixion, resurrection, ascension, and the day of Pentecost. The Gospel writer conveys nothing of their knowledge, experience, age, education, or status in society. Nothing they lack in human terms hinders their call to service. The only important factor is that Christ called and they went.

2. These missionaries were told they would be outnumbered, opposed by more powerful forces in the world, and would not have the resources they might have thought they needed. Clearly, these challenges required them to pray and trust in God's presence and provision. It is also a reminder that this is God's mission—not ours or the church's—and that we can be effective when we know ourselves to be participating in what God is doing in the world.

3. These "wolves" can be physical dangers to the lives of the seventy, such as the opposition the early Christians faced in Acts. Today we might encounter people among those we serve who face the "wolves" of disease, poverty, unemployment, homelessness, civil war, political oppression, sexual slavery, and the like. We will need to face the fact that our home environment has its own "wolves" that affect the way we see the world (for example, corporate or governmental greed and corruption).

4. Jesus invites them to trust that God will meet their needs and be in a relationship of mutual dependence when in mission. These are both important for our work today. What we bring to mission is not as important as who God is and what God is already doing. Our "stuff" often blinds us to that fact. Placing ourselves in the hands of strangers creates a better relationship with them than if we were self-sufficient and in charge. It is often much easier for us to be the host than to be the guest or the stranger. We must learn to be both.

5. In this situation, Jesus invites these proto-missionaries to enter into relationships with people, not to focus on events, presentations, or speeches. Their effectiveness resides in their ability to come alongside others, get to know them, depend upon them for sustenance and safety, and pay attention to their concerns and their needs.

6. It is a challenge for us to focus on the meal as more than physical sustenance. In many cultures the meal is about relationship, creating community, building trust,

inviting the outsider to the table, and caring for the stranger. It urges us to pay more attention to one another so that we can truly connect with others.

7. Luke's Gospel records Jesus eating with others on ten occasions. The stories around these meals comprise about 20 percent of Luke. The meals Jesus shares with others have significance for the work of the gospel: evangelism, reconciliation, service, teaching, justice, inclusiveness, gratitude, community building, a sign and foretaste of God's reign. We can do more good by eating together than we realize and more damage to our witness and relationships when we ignore the power of sharing a meal together.

8. As a starting point, the seventy are to offer God's peace to the households with whom they engage. This unconditional offer of God's presence does not depend upon the recipient's worth—only on his or her willingness to receive it. Their work is to build relationships (around meals especially), offer prayers, and place all of this in the context of God's reign. Their lives give witness to the authenticity of God's reign. The gospel must be congruent with who they are and how they live.

9. The seventy are to understand that this work is not about them or what they think they can accomplish. Jesus assumes their ability to do significant things; it is why he entrusted them with this mission in the first place. He wants them to see that they can undertake this mission because of their connection to him and because they trust him like a child. While our own learning, experience, and skills are valuable, they are not the source of our power. This is true of every Christian serving God's mission each day and everywhere, at home and far away.

10. This is the only place in the Gospels that the emotion of joy is noted in relation to Jesus. He expresses exuberant joy at ordinary followers discovering they can do extraordinary things for the kingdom. These disciples now know they are sent by God, working under the authority of Jesus, and empowered by the Spirit. This allows them to participate at the heart of God's activity and purpose in the world.

11. Scripture never implies that studying and learning is bad. On the contrary, scripture encourages us to apply our minds to God's word and understanding God's world. The danger comes when we put our trust in what we now know and not in the ultimate authority of God and what God continues to do in us. Our faith is not illogical in the face of what we might learn, but it remains beyond what we now see and understand, requiring us to seek God and trust in what God will make known.

12. Although we are imagining here, is it not likely that the seventy now paid more attention to the words and witness of Jesus? Surely they would have interpreted their experience in light of what Jesus continued to teach and do. Maybe they realized that they could continue with the same activities they did on their mission right where they were. Their newly discovered effectiveness might have become a part of their ongoing life as followers of Jesus, which, in turn, would have equipped them for the next time they were sent out on a specific mission.

ENGAGING IN GROUP CONVERSATION

Jane P. Ives

Encouraging individuals to reflect on and share their thoughts and feelings with others stimulates learning and personal growth. Effective team leaders and spiritual guides resist the temptation to tell participants what they ought to think and feel; instead they encourage them to reflect, share, and listen to one another. By asking open-ended questions, encouraging expressions of multiple points of view, and teaching and modeling active and empathic listening, leaders facilitate the deeper understanding of self and other that is the central purpose of group conversation.

Active listening involves feeding back what we hear another person say before we express an idea of our own. Empathic listening moves beyond active listening to suggest what the speaker might be feeling. Compassionate curiosity can help us attempt to understand the point of view of another, even when ours is different. We do not need to give up our convictions, only our belief that we alone have the truth and everyone else must agree with us, or else. Such dogmatic attitudes create enemies, making cooperation and peacemaking difficult, if not impossible. Telling people what they should or should not feel usually causes them to cling more defensively to what they believe. Criticizing or ridiculing what persons say will likely discourage them and others from further participation. Marshall Rosenberg, creator and developer of Nonviolent Communication and author of *Nonviolent Communication: A Language of Life*, teaches the power of expressing empathy, whether or not we agree with what we are hearing. He points out that persons are more likely to listen to someone when they know they have been heard.[2]

In addition to creating a group atmosphere in which persons feel comfortable expressing their opinions, effective leaders make sure everyone has a chance to participate. They not only prevent the more verbal members from monopolizing the conversation, but they also find ways to encourage active engagement by those less comfortable speaking in group situations. When you invite different persons to read the scripture passages and reflection and response suggestions during group processing of the meditations, they hear their own voices and may more easily contribute to the discussion. Another strategy involves giving everyone time to think and write down some thoughts before verbal sharing begins. Larger groups can be broken into groups of two or three for initial sharing, with or without time for written responses. Watch the clock during breakout sessions and remind the groups when it is time to hear from another speaker. It is important for everyone to have a turn to speak. If small-group participants are to report on their conversations, offer clear instructions beforehand; for example, "Listen for one or two things you want to share with the larger group."

In large-group conversations, ask a variety of open-ended, positively-focused questions, beginning with some that are relatively simple and objective. You may hope for your group sessions at the end of each day to become like John Wesley's class meetings in which participants respond to questions such as, "How is it with your soul?" Starting with less threatening questions, however, will encourage more participation. "What surprised you today?" "What was fun?" "What was hard?" "What made you laugh?" Once participants have engaged with the conversation and heard themselves speak, they may more likely contribute to deeper reflections. See pages 90–91 for suggested questions for these sessions. Always give participants the option to say "pass," especially if you are taking turns around the circle. Structuring a random order for conversation motivates participants to listen to what others are saying instead of thinking about how they will respond when it is their turn.

Eric Law's "Conversation by Mutual Invitation" allows everyone to share without feeling pressure to do so. The discussion leader either speaks first or designates someone else to give the first response to a question or topic. That person then invites another person to share. The person can share or pass, but must then invite another person to speak. This pattern continues until everyone has spoken or passed. The leader may need to remind each speaker of the freedom to pass and of the need to invite the next speaker.[3] Hearing their own voices helps even shy members of the group feel more comfortable participating in the conversation. Popcorn-style responses (inviting people to speak at random) creates a livelier dynamic. Other approaches include the use of a "talking stick," or some other object, which is held by the speaker and passed on to someone else when he or she is finished. Tossing a ball of yarn or soft foam object from person to person is another way to keep the conversation flowing smoothly. For more information on circle process, see chapter 5 of Thomas Porter's *The Spirit and Art of Conflict Transformation: Creating a Culture of JustPeace.*[4]

Before your mission journey, help the team create a behavioral covenant for your time together. Be sure to include expectations for group conversations: honor confidentiality, speak from your own experience, and do not put yourself or others down. Include insights gained from the cultural sensitivity exercises used during team training. Discuss what it means to function as a team, making individual decisions with consideration for their impact on everyone else. Agree on clear boundaries for sexual behavior, use of alcohol, drugs, tobacco products, and anything else that might cause problems or reflect badly on the team. Develop signals (when someone says, "I have a concern," the group will stop whatever it is doing in order to address that concern) and backup plans (someone who gets separated from the group waits in place to be found by the others). Remind the group that sometimes the team leader and host may have to make a decision for safety concerns or other reasons that will have to be explained at a later time. Discussing these issues in advance can help prevent problems later on and equips the team to deal with whatever happens.

As team leader or spiritual guide, your directions, questions, and responses set the tone for group discussions and behavior. Start and end group gatherings with spiritual centering and prayer. Listen with empathy, even when you disagree with what is being said. Resist the impulse to fix problems or give advice, except in emergency situations. In some cases, you may want to invite an individual or individuals for private discussion of an issue. Give participants time to explore their feelings and needs fully and challenge them to come up with their own solutions to problems. Above all, model confidence, curiosity, compassion, and kindness, striving diligently to create an atmosphere in which each person feels valued and loved.

"Is your heart as true to mine as mine is to yours? . . . If it is, give me your hand" (2 Kings 10:15).

SPIRITUAL CENTERING
A HANDOUT FOR PARTICIPANTS

Essential to any spiritual practice is the ability to focus, to calm both mind and body, and to connect to Christ within, the Holy Spirit, or whatever name we give the spiritual power available to each of us. Some of us may already have developed an active and reliable prayer life and deep spirituality, or we may just be beginning to discover the power of prayer and the ability to use our thoughts to override our instinctive reactions to people and events. Centering is the act of tuning out distractions, paying attention to what is going on inside us, and letting God speak to and through us. It is like tuning in to God's radio station or plugging ourselves into the power source. Spiritual centering often involves a conscious resolve to surrender to God's will, rather than let external events or internal stress control us.

Mission experiences offer an excellent opportunity for persons gathered for a common purpose to deepen their spiritual practice and to feel the power of the Holy Spirit. Prayer, at its most effective, is our intentional connection to the Source, allowing us to receive spiritual energy as well as channel it to others. Whatever words we might offer—words of thanks or words of petition—our prayers involve opening ourselves to the inflow of spiritual power and sometimes its outflow as well.

When Jesus taught his disciples about prayer he said, "Go into your room and shut the door and pray to your Father who is in secret" (Matt. 6:6). Many of us find it easier to pray and focus on God when we are in a space dedicated to that purpose—a church sanctuary or chapel, for example, or a specific place in our homes. But do we have to go somewhere physically to pray, or is it possible to simply focus inside ourselves? We know that Jesus often retreated to a deserted place to pray (Mark 1:35) or to a garden (Matt. 26:36), but we also observe from his words and actions that he stayed in close and constant communication with God, a practice Paul would later describe as praying "without ceasing" (1 Thess. 5:17).

Various scientific studies have shown that prayer can change outcomes and shape perspectives, including those of the person praying. The answers to our prayers may not always be the answers we want. Sometimes circumstances may stay the same while changes take place in our own attitudes and ability to cope. Jesus modeled the power of surrendering prayer in the garden of Gethsemane when he said, "Father . . . not my will, but thine be done" (Luke 22:42, KJV). It suffices to say that more spiritual power is available than most of us realize.

Although we profess belief in the power of prayer, distractions, both internal and external, often interfere with our intention to pray and certainly with our resolve to "pray without ceasing." Our culture sanctifies busyness, multitasking, and accomplishment, and most of us commit to more responsibilities than we can possibly fulfill. Even when we do not have a full schedule, we may worry and feel anxious, indicating, according to Eckhart Tolle, author of *The Power of Now,* that we are living in either the past or the future instead of in the present moment.[5] One antidote for distraction is "mindfulness meditation," in which we think only about what we are doing, savoring the sensual aspects of doing the dishes, for example, the warmth of the water, the smell of the soap, the gleam of light reflected off a clean plate. Or we might focus on "not doing," on simply being, noticing our breath and physical sensations in our bodies, calmly observing any random thoughts and feelings that arise and then letting them go.

We can use our minds to relax our bodies or we can use our bodies to relax our minds. Perhaps you have already participated in a guided meditation, closing your eyes and letting your thoughts be guided by a speaker who invites you to visualize a favorite place in nature, a person, or an art object that triggers relaxation and a spiritual connection to God. Or perhaps you have been led through a physical relaxation process such as tightening and then releasing muscle groups. In either case you may have felt the power of what Dr. Herbert Benson describes as the "relaxation response."[6] Meditation has moved into mainstream media through medical studies and self-help literature, where it is often presented without religious language. Sometimes we forget its sacred roots. Historically, however, many spiritual leaders have taught meditation—sometimes called contemplation—as the means for knowing and communing with God. In the early sixteenth century, Saint Ignatius of Loyola developed a set of Spiritual Exercises, a guide to meditation and prayer designed to help persons draw closer to God.[7] In the seventeenth century, Brother Lawrence, a French monk, spoke of "practicing the presence of God" in order to become more aware of God's ever-present love and guidance.[8] More recently, Jon Kabat-Zinn has incorporated Buddhist teachings in his accessible books about meditation.[9]

Christians in the sixth century were taught to draw closer to God by praying continuously, "Lord Jesus Christ, have mercy on me." Often called The Jesus Prayer, this prayer and variations of it inspired *The Breath of Life: A Simple Way to Pray*. This book invites individuals to form a personal breath prayer by choosing a word to address God as they inhale and words of petition to accompany their exhale. One might breathe in "Loving God" and breathe out "Show me the way," or "Holy One, grant me your peace."[10]

As with any new habit, only consistent and regular practice over time will establish spiritual centering as an automatic response. Choose and practice a centering discipline for use BEFORE, DURING, and AFTER your mission experience. This could be a brief prayer, a verse of scripture, a deep cleansing breath, a mental image (such as the cross or the face of Jesus), or a peaceful natural setting. Repeat the word or words, action, mental image, or combination of these frequently and regularly until centering becomes a habit. Practice this while waiting in line, completing a task that requires no thought, or when you feel stressed or weary to spark a sense of closeness to God. Spiritual centering, practiced faithfully, can transform every aspect of your life.

"Draw near to God and [God] will draw near to you"
(James 4:8, NKJV).

BEFORE

. . . .

THE MISSION EXPERIENCE

INTRODUCTION

Preparation for a mission experience involves learning and sharing by everyone involved. The host team may be preoccupied with making arrangements at the site and the volunteer team may be distracted by making travel arrangements and packing. Even more important from a discipling point of view is the work both teams do to understand their cultural identities and attitudes and to prepare to develop partner relationships. Team leaders will want to schedule team member training sessions or find other ways to share information before the mission experience. Material is provided in this section for three such sessions. Team leaders may choose what they find most relevant and combine sessions as needed.

The volunteer team needs factual information about the mission site and its history, geography, and culture. The host team leader can guide the volunteer team leader to appropriate resources and help clarify the particular perspectives inherent in them. Likewise, the volunteer team leader can communicate helpful information to the host team leader about the visiting team and also inquire about previous experiences and concerns.

For the following activities, be sure each participant has a journal in which to record responses to the various reflection questions, as well as insights, feelings, questions, and concerns throughout the mission experience. Activities, including the meditations, that you would like individuals to complete before the first meeting may be duplicated and sent to team members, and those for the following sessions may be distributed at the end of the prior session. If you decide not to share the "Spiritual Centering Handout" (pages 53–55) in advance, be sure to distribute it at your first meeting.

You will also have practical matters to discuss during these sessions. For more information visit "Dos and Don'ts" on the Resources on Mission Volunteers website: http://www.umcmission.org/Get-Involved/Volunteer>. The suggestions found in "Engaging in Group Conversation" (pages 49–51) will also be valuable to you during this time, particularly when you begin to establish a behavioral covenant.

ANSWERING GOD'S CALL
MEDITATION BEFORE THE MISSION EXPERIENCE

SCRIPTURE

Then I heard the voice of the Lord saying, "Whom shall I send? And who will go for us?" And I said, "Here am I; send me!" (Isa. 6:8, NIV).

[Jesus] stood up to read. The scroll of the prophet Isaiah was handed to him. Unrolling it, he found the place where it is written: "The Spirit of the Lord is on me, because he has anointed me to preach good news to the poor . . . Today this scripture is fulfilled in your hearing" (Luke 4:18-21, NIV).

Again Jesus said, "Peace be with you! As the Father has sent me, I am sending you" (John 20:21, NIV).

REFLECTION

Why did you sign up for this experience? Are you looking for an adventure? Do you want to learn something? Meet new people? See the world from a different perspective? Find out what you can do in a challenging situation? Are you so moved by gratitude for what God has done and is doing in your life that you want to share God's love with others? Know that wherever you are going and for whatever reason, whether visiting or hosting, God is already at work there and calls you into a divine partnership. We go to be the hands and feet of Jesus, channels of God's love, in a specific place in a specific time. We must put aside our preconceived notions of the places and people we will encounter and open ourselves to new possibilities.

What are your reasons for taking part in this experience?

What are your hopes?

Read Jesus' mission statement from Luke in the second scripture passage listed above. Which phrase resonates with you most?

In what mission experiences have you participated before?

What do you expect to be similar this time?

What do you think will be different?

Think about your destination or about the area from which your volunteers are coming. What are your impressions of that place and of the persons who live there? What do you actually know about its geography, history, famous persons, and recent and current events?

How do you think your life might be different if you lived there?

How do you think God might be at work there?

What forces there do you think might work against God's will?

RESPONSE

Learn more about your destination (or the area from which your visitors are coming) through individual research and group sharing. Participate in activities that deepen your understanding of cultural awareness and justice issues (see pages 77–80). Make a covenant to pray daily for those who will share in the mission experience with you and for those who may benefit from your mission work.

PRAYER

Loving God, I accept your call to serve you in this mission. Open my eyes and my ears and my heart to discern and work for your will with the people we will meet and for the place where we will serve. I surrender to your will, that I may be transformed by this experience into a more effective disciple of Jesus Christ. *Amen.*

TEAM CULTURAL ACTIVITY

1. Guided reflection for mission volunteers on Luke 13:10-17.

Recalling the definition of the word *culture*, read the scripture passage in its entirety and identify which actions reflect the cultural practices and perspectives of the time.

What are the customary practices that Jesus challenges?

Did the leaders of the synagogue really not want the crippled woman to be healed or were they simply speaking from the perspective of custom?

Is there some possibility that the leaders of the synagogue were also reacting to the usefulness of Jesus?

Do you suppose Jesus did not know what the cultural customary practice was with regard to healing on the sabbath?

2. Team reflection on mission and culture (Luke 13:10-17).

Team members are invited to read the text from Luke and share their reflections on experiences from their own lives in which different practices of the church are questioned like they are in the story. Team members are invited to imagine a situation that challenges customary practices in their own church and then discuss their reflections and consider different possibilities for action.

Here is an example that may get you started. A church may offer a vacation Bible school where the children are drawn from families of members of the church. Suppose a new member of the congregation suggests that instead of serving children of the congregation, volunteers go into the poor neighborhood surrounding the church and recruit children from the community to attend. Would all members of the church embrace such a change?

Working in groups of three or four, team members might create a role-play based on this situation to help them think about what steps they would take when creating change and what kind of response they might receive.

As the final part of this activity, team members are asked to think about the task in which they will engage during the mission journey and whether similar cross-cultural perspectives may also occur.

SEARCH ME AND KNOW MY HEART
MEDITATION BEFORE THE MISSION EXPERIENCE

SCRIPTURE

After this the Lord appointed seventy others and sent them on ahead of him in pairs to every town and place where he himself intended to go. He said to them, "The harvest is plentiful, but the laborers are few; therefore ask the Lord of the harvest to send out laborers into his harvest" (Luke 10:1-2).

You did not choose me but I chose you. And I appointed you to go and bear fruit, fruit that will last, so that the Father will give you whatever you ask him in my name (John 15:16).

Search me, O God, and know my heart; test me and know my thoughts (Ps. 139:23).

REFLECTION

Each child of God possesses certain gifts. They may include obvious talents, such as carpentry, singing, or cooking, or they may be less obvious but equally important abilities, such as listening, understanding, and organizing. Each of us also has vulnerabilities and weaknesses—a tendency to act impulsively without considering others or the feeling that we must compete and be the best in all we do. Sometimes our weaknesses are our strengths taken to extremes, and our gifts may also be our burdens. For example, sensitivity to the feelings of others can make us compassionate. It can also make us feel insecure. Our vulnerabilities are gifts, as well as our graces, because they remind us of our dependence on God and offer us opportunities for growth.

What fears might the seventy followers of Jesus have felt when he sent them out?

What fears do you experience as you prepare for this mission journey?

How might you think differently about these fears in order to be less overwhelmed by them?

What gifts do you bring to this experience?

What vulnerabilities might cause you to need specific care or guidance?

What would help you most at such times?

RESPONSE

If you are leaving home or will be engaged in the mission experience for a period of time, make a list of persons to whom you want to speak loving words before you go, and plan when and how you will do so. Commend each of them to God's care. If you have unfinished business that will have to wait until your return, list these tasks or concerns and delegate them to someone else's care (if possible) while you are gone.

Share with your team members what you understand to be your gifts and vulnerabilities. Offer some ideas about how they might empower you to use your gifts and help you when your weaknesses come into play.

Participate thoughtfully in your team's development of a behavioral covenant. If you are uncomfortable about any part of it, speak up. If you think you might have difficulty honoring any part of the covenant others agree to, talk privately with your team leader or spiritual guide.

If you have not already done so, choose one of the centering prayer disciplines listed on pages 53–55 and practice it at least once each day (preferably more often) so that it becomes automatic for you. Use this discipline to meditate on God's love and to listen for God's guidance.

PRAYER

Loving God, fill me with confidence in your care and presence as I begin this journey. May I feel your joy when I do well and your grace when I make mistakes. Help me also to encourage others and to serve as a channel of your grace. In Jesus' name. *Amen.*

TEAM CULTURAL ACTIVITIES

Understanding Cultural Identities

One aspect of the mission experience is that it provides a place for growth, a place for openness to the possibility of transformation. In order for transformation to occur, it is important that the volunteers and hosts think ahead about their own cultural identities—who they are, what their attitudes are, what attitudes influence them, and what attitudes they have toward others with whom they will partner in the mission task. Cultural identity includes such characteristics as race, class, nationality, faith journey, geography, customary attitudes, values, and beliefs. For volunteers it also involves identifying comfort zones. Every culture has particular ways of functioning and particular attitudes toward the fundamental activities of life. While one culture's approach to life may be different from that of another, we should not assume that one way is necessarily better than another; the two ways are just different. A vital step in the volunteer's path is self-reflection in order to name some of the fundamental attitudes that may affect their experience in the mission context.

Understanding Attitudes and Realities

Because the mission experience is an encounter between cultures, the presence of preexisting attitudes is inevitable. Members of the volunteer team will have attitudes about the host context. These attitudes may be based upon factual information, misinformation, or conflicting information. They may also be based on stereotype and prejudice. The same is true for those in the host community. An important part of preparing for the mission experience is naming and sharing these attitudes.

TEAM ACTIVITY

1. Create a Cultural Identity page of your mission experience in your personal journal.

Write the names of three friends and then identify the ethnic/racial/class/national identity of each person.

Next, list your own ethnic/racial/class/national identity.

2. Reflect on the following questions, and record your responses in your journal.

What does this information tell you about yourself?

What does this information reveal about your experience with diversity? Has your experience been wide or narrow or somewhere in between?

How will this experience be a resource for you in the mission context, or will it be the beginning of the growth process?

Establishing a Personal Cultural Baseline through Journaling

As volunteers begin their mission journey, whether it is their first experience or the most recent of many, an important part of preparation is thinking about cultural starting points. The volunteers must ask, "Who am I and what are the cultural understandings that I will bring to this experience?" This will help the volunteer determine personal assets and liabilities for the tasks ahead. All levels of experience are affirmed as a starting point for learning and growth.

Uncovering Personal Comfort Spaces

Volunteers often find themselves in unfamiliar situations and places. An important part of preparation is to take time to reflect on those aspects of daily life that we often take for granted, but if they are missing they can make us feel uncomfortable or off-balance. Identifying some of these aspects before the journey begins can serve as a way to anticipate problems and find solutions before they arise. This is information that can be shared with other members of the volunteer team during orientation.

TEAM ACTIVITY

Create a Comfort Space page in your personal journal. Complete the following statements and record any reflections on your answers.

My reaction to unfamiliar **food** is to _____.

I am always _____ **time,** and I expect others to _____ **time.**

I am **sensitive as to how** _____ are treated, and I _____ on their behalf.

When I am in an **unfamiliar place** I feel
_____.

If I am surrounded by people speaking a different **language** I feel _____.

I want to go on the mission trip because I want to _____. (Select the one that best describes what you hope to do: **learn, teach**).

TEAM ACTIVITY

Guided discussion of comfort spaces

The team leader asks team members to refer to the Comfort Space page in their personal journals and to review their answers. Volunteers are asked to share one or two points from their responses. If the group is large, this activity can be done in small groups.

Personal Cultural Identity Profile

Jim names his Street High School friends: Brian who is a white middle-class boy from the United States. Mary, also white, comes from a working-class Italian family. Jim's best buddy, Vishal, comes from a family from India even though Vishal was born in the United States. His father is a pharmacist.

Jim is a white American, and his father owns a car dealership.

Jim has visited the homes of Mary and Brian, but he has never been to the home of Vishal. Jim concludes that most of what he knows about other countries comes from what he sees on television. This helps Jim realize that he has much to learn during his mission experience in Latin America.

Once everyone has had a chance to share, invite the group to construct a list (on newsprint or screen) of issues around comfort space that they would like to talk about. Prioritize the issues for discussion.

Following the discussion, ask the group to suggest ways in which they might function collectively to support one another and ease some of the adjustment issues. The discussion should conclude with the establishment of procedures and division of responsibilities in dealing with the issues once the team is in the mission context.

Recognizing Comfort Spaces

The process of coping in a new environment is not just a task for each team member. It can be an important shared responsibility that builds and strengthens the team and its work. The orientation is a place for sharing information about comfort spaces for the development of collective strategies. The discussion can give volunteers with more experience a chance to share their learning with team members who may be beginning their first experience.

National Identity and Attitudes

Volunteers bring their national identity with them to the mission experience. This identity is often felt most sharply when we are in a new and different national context. Viewing our nation or community from the outside can be revealing. A substantial part of preparation for the mission experience is naming some of these elements before the journey. Naming them gives the volunteer a head start on developing new understandings about the role of national identity in the mission task. Once volunteers are in the mission context they can listen for the comparable perspectives of those in the host country.

TEAM ACTIVITY

Create a National Identity and Attitudes page in your personal journal. Complete the following statements and record any reflections on your answers.

I believe my country is _____.

I am most proud of my country for _____.

When I compare my country to other countries I _____.

The most important social justice issues in my country are _____.

The biggest justice challenges in the world today are _____.

Understanding Attitudes

Team members and persons from the host community enter the mission experience with preconceived notions about one another. It is important in preparing for the mission experience that the team members have an opportunity to share with the group these preconceived ideas.

══════════ TEAM ACTIVITY ══════════

1. Naming and acknowledging attitudes toward the host community and volunteers

The team leader invites each volunteer to list five characteristics or attitudes they have about the host country (for example, poor, few resources).

The team leader shares with the group the list of five characteristics that persons in the host country perceive those from the volunteer country having (see examples below).

The team leader shares the five most critical aspects the host believes volunteers should know about the host context before arriving.

Team members discuss the contrast between these lists and begin to think about how they might overcome the negative attitudes they may encounter in the host country.

The team may want to create role-play dialogues that address these issues (see examples on the next page).

The leader should share with the group information from the host about the important customs of the mission context that volunteers will need to know in order to help them in the new environment.

2. Seeing ourselves as others see us

The team leader can share the list of host community attitudes and reflections about volunteers and the volunteers' home country based on their experience with other volunteers and their overall general experience. Here is a sample list compiled from comments received from hosts in several countries.

Volunteers are
- pushy and projects-focused
- loud and arrogant
- demanding
- unaware of the impact of their own wealth
- unknowledgeable about the history and customs of our country and do not know that our country is a world leader in new ethanol technologies
- insincere when it comes to learning about other cultures
- quick to want to talk about their own country and share stories of their own country
- naïve
- confident they have an answer to every problem and know the best ways to fix them
- quick to offer money as a solution
- always asking questions about how things are customarily done

Team Discussion and Reflection Worksheet

1. Which of these characteristics seem most likely to be true as seen through the eyes of an outsider?

2. Which of these characteristics are most surprising?

3. Which of these characteristics might offer the most difficulty for the volunteers in the mission context?

4. Which of these attitudes could the team work together to change?

5. What steps could be taken to address these attitudes?

An additional team activity BEFORE the mission experience can be found in the first exercise on page 93, "A Meal Is More Than a Menu."

THEY WILL KNOW WE ARE CHRISTIANS BY OUR LOVE
MEDITATION BEFORE THE MISSION EXPERIENCE

SCRIPTURE

For as in one body we have many members, and not all the members have the same function, so we, who are many, are one body in Christ, and individually we are members one of another. We have gifts that differ according to the grace given to us: prophecy, in proportion to faith; ministry, in ministering; the teacher, in teaching; the exhorter, in exhortation; the giver, in generosity; the leader, in diligence; the compassionate, in cheerfulness (Rom. 12:4-8).

Let love be genuine; hate what is evil, hold fast to what is good; love one another with mutual affection; outdo one another in showing honor (Rom. 12:9-10).

REFLECTION

Competition seems to be deeply rooted in our culture. Perhaps it's even in our DNA. When we feel insecure, especially in new situations, we often find ourselves looking around at other persons, secretly wondering if we measure up. When the disciples argued about which of them was the greatest, Jesus said, "Whoever wants to be first must be last of all and servant of all" (Mark 9:35). Our calling is to serve others, not to try to earn God's love, which is, in fact, already ours. Those of us who grew up without experiencing unconditional love may strive to earn acceptance and approval, but God's love already belongs to us.

Another characteristic deeply rooted in our culture is the tendency to judge and criticize, perhaps in a misguided effort to prove ourselves equal or even superior to others. Jesus was clear when he said, "Do not judge, so that you may not be judged" (Matt.

7:1). When we judge others we indict ourselves, for we are often intolerant of qualities in others that we struggle with in ourselves. If we can get beyond competitiveness and judgment and recognize how much alike we all are, we can confidently affirm the uniqueness and mystery of all people, including ourselves.

Marshall Rosenberg, in his teaching and writing on nonviolent communication, asserts that our behavior at any given time is an effort to meet needs of which we may or may not be aware.[1] Needs are universal. If we are not clear about our needs, we may make choices that work against our needs being met. If we are feeling the need for connection but feel hurt by someone else's behavior, we might lash out in anger and drive them further from us. On the other hand, if we can express interest in and concern for others, we might learn that their behavior had nothing to do with us but came out of a need within the other person. Rosenberg teaches us to listen with empathy and to seek to understand others before we offer a different point of view or express our own feelings and needs.[2]

Think of a time when you felt deeply and unconditionally loved, or think of someone who loves you this way. If no examples come to mind, try to imagine what it would be like to have someone who loves you in such a way that you know he or she would never abandon you. What words would you use to describe this experience?

Think of a time when you felt rejected, bullied, or abandoned, or think of someone who treated you this way. Consider your wounded self with empathy. Ask yourself what you need in order to heal from this wound.

Now think of that same hurtful experience again, but instead of dwelling on your own painful feelings, try to imagine what might have been going on inside the other person that caused him or her to act the way he or she did. What need might have been driving that behavior?

RESPONSE

Think about the other members of your team. Resolve to put aside any judgments or assumptions you have made about them and to approach them with compassion and curiosity. Formulate questions you can ask to learn more about who they are, what they feel, and what they need. Consider what it might mean for you to act as a caring servant toward your fellow team members, both individually and collectively.

If you are a volunteer, think about your hosts who have invited you to come and who are preparing for your arrival. If you are a host, think about those who will be your guests. Resolve to set aside any judgments or assumptions you have made about them and meet them with an open mind and heart. Know that they, like you, want to love and be loved, and that they may feel anxious about making a good impression on you. Consider the qualities of a gracious host or a gracious guest, whichever role you play. Mentally rehearse how to live out that role to the glory of God.

Prayerfully center yourself and imagine God's spirit, like the dove at the baptism of Jesus, blessing each member of your team and the hosts (or volunteers) with whom you will share this experience. Hear God's voice affirming each person, "This is my [son/daughter], in whom I am well pleased" (Matt. 3:17).

PRAYER

Loving God, you are both our gracious host and a welcome guest in our lives. Open us to the needs of others, and grant us both the will and the wisdom to serve them as Jesus taught us to do. *Amen.*

TEAM CULTURAL AND JUSTICE ACTIVITIES

Diversity Experience

Another aspect of the mission experience is the volunteer's history with diversity. For many first-time volunteers and new hosts, the mission experience may mean encountering persons who are different from those in their home community. This experience is the starting point of the mission encounter. It is knowledge that can help the volunteer team have a better understanding of how to work together. It is also knowledge that can help the team leader and the host leader in their planning for the mission experience. This knowledge is not about judgment, and it helps for both host and mission volunteers to measure changes and transformation in cultural awareness BEFORE, DURING, and AFTER the mission experience.

1. Exploring Team Diversity

Because many team members will be in a new cultural context, a primary task is to think about their collective experience in situations of diversity. This moving-line exercise can help team members assess and demonstrate their experience graphically, and it provides a good opportunity for reflection.

The team leader invites members of the team to form a line across the center of the room. Ask volunteers to think about a situation where they have encountered persons that are different from themselves and then to take:

- Three steps forward if the encounter was one of close friendship
- Two steps backward if the encounter was a casual acquaintance
- Three steps backward if impersonal (a business or service relationship)
- Four steps backward if there are no experiences with difference

After each movement, ask team members to look around and see where other members of the team are. Repeat the exercise one or two more times. At the end of the activity, the team leader asks members of the team to assess their personal readiness and the team's readiness for encountering situations of difference and diversity based upon this exercise.

Discussion will focus on what the exercise reveals about the team's collective experiences with diversity. Has the team's experiences with cultural diversity been deep and rich, superficial and impersonal, or somewhere in between?

Team members can assess the team's readiness for encountering situations of diversity based upon this exercise. Team members use this information to begin to articulate team goals for mutuality and building relationships within the mission experience.

2. Watch the video "Who Am I?" Follow with group discussion.

"Who Am I?" Rev. Eric H. F. Law of the Kaleidoscope Institute, Los Angeles, CA. The video can be found on YouTube at http://www.youtube.com/watch?v=lP_Ia0Zitdg

Understanding and Seeking Justice

A clear biblical imperative identifies the task of people of faith as joining in God's works on behalf of justice to feed the hungry, clothe the naked, and set at liberty those who are oppressed. For the mission volunteer, this is exciting and complex territory. In this time of globalization we can comprehend the interconnectedness of our lives. What people in a rich country choose to eat or choose not to eat, wear or not wear, may profoundly effect the ability of people in another part of the world to survive. Adverse weather or economic conditions in one part of the world can have a ripple effect and create hardship around the globe. Who wins and who loses in a global economy is not a matter of chance, it is a matter of justice. As volunteers enter the mission context, it is crucial that they bring with them some basic understandings of global realities— knowledge of key justice issues in their own country as well as other countries and an awareness of their attitudes toward these issues. Some volunteers will also need to be aware that they bring with them a national/racial identity that reflects the national/racial identity of the majority and the history of the relationships between their country and the host country or community, a history that will not always be positive. The volunteer must think clearly about what constitutes appropriate action for justice as a visitor in a nation or community.

Mission cannot be separated from God's justice. God's justice lies at the heart of mission. Volunteers bring a variety of understandings to the meaning of the word *justice*. They may or may not connect the tasks of the mission context to justice.

TEAM ACTIVITY

Sharing perspectives on justice is a key part of the team's collective preparation for the mission experience.

The team leader should ask team members to reflect on their responses on the National Identity and Attitudes page in their journal, particularly questions 4 and 5. Invite team members to share their responses to these two questions. If the group is large, you may wish to form small groups. If forming small groups, ask one member of each group to record the group's responses. The group then responds to any or all of the following questions:

- Why do you think this issue is important?
- What do you think needs to be done?
- How do you think the church is (can be) involved?

- What does work on this issue have to do with your understanding of mission?
- How do you see the work of your mission trip contributing to the work of justice?

DEDICATION SERVICES FOR VOLUNTEERS AND HOSTS

Dedication services for sending mission teams forth are most meaningful when they are held within the community of faith from which persons come, whether for volunteers or host communities. The community might be an annual conference, district, cooperative parish, local church, or some other organization or location. Including the dedication as part of a service or event already scheduled may ensure that more persons participate. The primary factor is for the mission experience to be celebrated and understood as part of the ongoing life of the faith community.

At the very least, dedication services should include three parts:

- An opening statement explaining the purpose of the mission experience
- A challenge to the participants
- A response by the community of faith

The opening statement might include words spoken by Jesus, such as John 15:9, John 15:16, and Mark 16:15. A brief general statement on mission, perhaps from denominational resources, could be followed by a few sentences about the specific destination of the team or teams that are being dedicated. Because our understanding of mission has evolved over time, we suggest the following sentences—or others to the same effect—be included in the opening statement:

> *The task of mission is to establish and nurture partner relationships that empower us to work together on behalf of God's purposes. Mission involves the encounter of different cultures, different national histories, different political systems and practices, different levels of wealth and power, different mission histories, and different spiritual and faith understandings. Each person involved in the mission experience serves at the intersection of all these differences. Understanding these elements of the mission context will play a critical role for all those involved*

as we work together to understand how to answer God's call, how to deepen our self-understanding and connection to God, and how to live so that others will "know we are Christians by our love."

A simple challenge to team members might read as follows:

Leader: Do you sincerely believe that you have been led by the Spirit of God to engage in this ministry?

Response: I do so believe.

Leader: Will you earnestly seek to carry forward this mission in a Christlike manner, in cooperation with your fellow team members and leaders, and with full respect for national church officials and local hosts?

Response: I will, the Lord being my helper.[3]

Team members are then invited to kneel while the minister and congregation pray for them. In some cultures, the liturgist might invite persons from the community of faith to lay hands on those being dedicated. The following prayer is one example. It is based on a prayer from the Southeastern Jurisdiction UMVIM *Team Leader Handbook.*[4]

Almighty God, whose love for the whole family of humankind has been made known to us through your Son, send your blessings upon these your servants, soon to go forth on this mission endeavor. Guide and strengthen them for their task, open their minds and hearts to new truths and insights, and bless them with good health and traveling mercies. May this mission experience glorify you and bring our world closer to your reign on the earth. In the name of Jesus and in the power of the Holy Spirit. Amen.

At this time, the faith community covenants to pray for the team members while they are engaged in the mission experience and to support them by caring for the families and work they leave behind:

We covenant to pray for you daily while you are engaged in this mission experience and to care for your loved ones and the commitments you leave behind. We will await your return with eager anticipation of all you will have to share, and we pledge our support for the ongoing mission experience as it unfolds over time. Amen.

The team and the congregation then sings a hymn together, such as "Here I Am, Lord" (*UMH*, no. 593) or another hymn that speaks of answering God's call, going out to serve, and committing to follow Christ.

Using the same dedication or sending forth service for both volunteers and hosts sets a common tone and helps to nurture the bond between them. Creative use of symbols can add drama to the service and make it more memorable. A UMVIM group from the West Ohio Conference developed a "mantling" service based on Elijah's passing of his mantle to Elisha (2 Kings 2:8-15). After reading or telling the story, the leader holds up pieces of cloth, perhaps just small scraps, saying, "Today, we place these mantles on you as a sign of your commissioning for this service. Others have come before; others will follow after. During this mission, you are chosen as servants of God. These mantles are to remind you of the presence of the Holy Spirit to empower, protect, and inspire you. Wear them as reminders of the love of the church that sends you and that Christ has chosen you to make his glory known in others." Alternatively, the leader might read the story of Jesus washing the feet of his disciples in John 13:1-11 and remind the participants that they go into this mission experience to serve as the hands of Jesus.[5]

The 2005 edition of the Southeastern Jurisdiction's *Handbook for United Methodist Volunteers in Mission* includes a sending forth service based on the traditional belief that a covenant sealed with salt is a promise made before God never to be broken. Tasting a small portion of salt, the participants remember Jesus' call to be "the salt of the earth" (Matt. 5:13). In another ritual, "The Peace Candle Ceremony," the team members receive a candle to take with them to use in a peace prayer ceremony and to present to those with whom they will share the experience.[6] Let these examples inspire your creativity as you weave symbols representing the place you come from and/or the place where you are going (or some other aspect of the experience that will have special meaning for the participants) into the service.

DURING

. . . .

THE MISSION EXPERIENCE

INTRODUCTION

Once the volunteer team has arrived in the mission context and started its work, focus shifts to listening, learning, and reflecting on all aspects that were part of the team's preparation: biblical reflection (Answering God's Call); cultural baseline (Search Me and Know Me); comfort spaces, attitudes, and diversity experiences and justice (They Will Know We Are Christians by Our Love).

Part of the exciting opportunity of mission is the meeting between volunteers and hosts. This involves intentional work, such as naming the cultural experiences of the mission context. It also involves problem solving related to those experiences that play an integral part to the life of the volunteer team. Probably all of these tasks will be present whether the mission experience is three days or three weeks.

These tasks require the participation of all team members, including the team leader and hosts. The team leader and host will have discussed possible places and times for conversation as part of their planning process. The team leader and other persons agreed upon by the team take responsibility for working on particular problems or creating systems within the team to address issues that may arise.

An equally important activity as the mission experience draws to a close is preparing for reentry into the volunteer's home context. This involves thinking about what differences the mission experience will make in the volunteer's day-to-day life. Preparations for reentry include discussion of ongoing relationships with those from the mission context, ways to share the mission experience back home, and strategies for the team's ongoing support and connection to one another.

CULTIVATING SPIRITUAL TRANSFORMATION

Team leaders and spiritual guides have developed a variety of rituals and practices designed to create a spiritually nourishing atmosphere for mission experiences. Worship can set the tone for a team's time together, encourage a positive group attitude, and help team members through rough spots. Volunteers are usually invited to participate in a service planned and led by the hosts, and volunteers frequently invite the hosts to worship with them. In addition to these scheduled events, worship moments woven into the team experience can even more effectively nurture spiritual transformation. These moments might include brief periods of prayer, song, or quiet reflection. Rituals may be preplanned or spring spontaneously out of the group's life together. If well-prepared and intuitive, both volunteer and host team leaders and spiritual guides can take advantage of moments to acknowledge dependence on and gratitude to God, modeling the integration of faith into daily life.

Leaders can prepare their team members for the experience of worshiping in a style different from that to which they are accustomed. Visiting volunteers might benefit from knowing ahead of time that services led by their hosts may be longer than those back home, as well as more lively, and they may include multiple offerings and/or the practice of each person dancing forward with his or her gifts. Hosts will appreciate orientation, pre-teaching of hymns or songs, and explanation of such rituals as "passing the peace." In both situations, basic hospitality includes telling participants ahead of time what they need to know in order to understand what is happening.

Mission experiences offer numerous occasions to acknowledge the Holy and incorporate prayer into ordinary, daily experiences. Host drivers often invite their passengers to join them in a prayer for safe travel before setting out on their journey. Sometimes teams sing the same hymn or song each morning, perhaps "This Is the Day" (*UMH*, no. 657) or "Rise and Shine" (http://www.metrolyrics.com/rise-and-shine-lyrics-children. html), or different persons might choose and lead a wake-up song each day. Volunteer and host teams can take turns planning and leading a brief time of worship before beginning work each day. Teams can use the same prayer before breakfast, lunch, and dinner, or different team members might offer a prayer or lead a song before each meal. Even snack time can be prefaced with a simple call and response, such as "For these mercies . . . we thank you, God." During group prayers, whoever expresses a celebration or concern can conclude with "This is my prayer." The group then responds with the affirmation, "This is our prayer."

The spiritual centering practices described on pages 53–55 can deeply influence both individual and group responses to whatever happens. We do not have to let what happens to us control us, because God gives us the power to choose how we will respond to any given situation. Most of us react to certain triggers in ways we have learned over time, and self-knowledge about these triggers can help us rise above our own reactivity and choose more helpful responses. The three meditations in the section titled, "Search

Me and Know Me" (BEFORE, DURING, and AFTER, pages 65, 101, and 131) are designed to help persons reflect on their own vulnerabilities and strengths with self-empathy. Learning to take a deep cleansing breath before responding to a challenging person or event, using a breath prayer, or reciting a line from a hymn or passage of scripture can empower us to behave in a more Christlike manner. When waiting for a driver or for supplies to show up, singing a hymn such as "Have Thine Own Way, Lord" (*UMH*, no. 382) or "We Are the Church" (*UMH*, no. 558) or even a campfire-type song can help team members fend off impatience and maintain a positive attitude. While engaged in a mundane task such as moving bricks by passing them from person to person, a lively song can keep everyone's spirits up and provide inspiration.

While on site, volunteers and hosts can participate together in the three meditations for DURING the mission experience (pages 97, 101, and 113), perhaps at the end of the day or use them separately, depending on the schedule and other factors. These meditations will be more meaningful if both teams have completed the three meditations for BEFORE the mission experience (pages 61, 65, and 75).

Daily reflection and group processing at the end of each day is essential to nurturing the spiritual formation and transformation of team members. See pages 90–91 for specific suggestions. You will also want to review "Engaging in Group Conversation" (pages 49–51), since participants will learn and benefit most by actively participating in this, as well as other group sessions.

Encouraging participants to journal about their experiences and to record their thoughts and questions on events will result in deeper reflection and insight and nurture spiritual growth. Some groups keep a team journal by assigning either one person to record each day's events or a different person each day. Another option is to provide a journal and leave it open in a common place so that anyone can write in it whenever he or she feels so moved. The team journal, with the addition of pictures taken during the mission experience, may be copied and distributed to each participant afterward as a lasting reminder of the mission experience.

Often during a mission experience the host team will plan an outing or celebration for volunteer guests. Although visiting volunteers may feel guilty about spending time this way and about the possible cost to the hosts, they need to understand how important it is for the hosts to share something of their culture, the natural beauty of their geographical setting, and/or the unique talents of their people. This act of hospitality is blessed when guests participate and receive the gift with genuine appreciation.

Early in the mission experience, some volunteer team leaders might encourage their members to think about leaving something small and unobtrusive behind to symbolize how they have become part of a new place. Volunteers can write their names on a wall before covering it with insulation and paneling. Others may bury a small piece of cloth in wet cement. Do this only after consultation with the hosts. This caution also applies to any mementos volunteers may want to take with them when they leave.

A worshipful mission experience and a team life infused with moments of inspiration and spiritual guidance will cultivate the spiritual formation and transformation of the participants, helping to make them truly "disciples of Jesus Christ for the transformation of the world."[1]

DAILY REFLECTION AND GROUP PROCESSING

Daily group processing, essential for cultivating spiritual transformation, helps thoughts and feelings surface that might otherwise go unexpressed and unexplored. If teams are small, hosts and volunteers might come together for this experience, or team leaders and spiritual guides may decide that separate gatherings would encourage deeper sharing. In either case, be sure to read "Engaging in Group Conversation" for ideas to maximize participation (pages 49-51).

The following groups of questions are arranged in ascending order of difficulty to help you begin the conversation at a more comfortable level.

QUESTIONS TO HELP INTERPRET THE DAY

What was good?
What was fun?
What was challenging?
What surprised you?
What was something new you learned?
What made you laugh?
What annoyed you?
What made you sad?

Where did you experience cultural differences?
What challenged you?
What did you struggle with today?
When did you use your spiritual centering prayer discipline?
When might you have benefited from doing so?

When did you experience hope?
When did you experience discouragement and/or failure?
Where did you witness suffering and death?
Where did you witness life and joy?
Where did you experience poverty? abundance?
What might be at the root of these disparities?

Where did you experience or witness God's grace?
Where did you encounter Jesus offering comfort and care?
Where did you encounter Jesus challenging or confronting?
How were you Jesus to others?
What scripture passages or hymns speak to your experiences?

For questions related to justice issues, see the Team Activity on page 117.

Reflections on the day's experiences can lead to a time of shared prayer. Invite members of the group to assume a posture of prayer—heads bowed and/or holding hands. Encourage individuals to complete the prayer prompt "popcorn-style."

For what do we thank God today?
For whom or what do we ask God's guidance and help?
What concerns do we need to release into God's hands?

Another approach to shared prayer is to ask for joys and concerns, inviting partic-ipants to conclude what they share with the words, "This is my prayer." The group then responds with the affirmation, "This is our prayer."

A MEAL IS MORE THAN A MENU
AN ACTIVITY IN THE CULTURE OF FOOD

Jeremy Basset

Sharing a meal involves more than the food we consume. In many societies the emphasis lies on the presentation, choice, variety, cost, and setting of the food that is consumed. But meals reflect more than consumption. They reflect a community's culture—and even their theology, spirituality, and issues of justice.

When we share a meal with people from another culture, the differences in our approach to food often raise stark cultural differences. Some of these differences might frighten us (exactly what we are eating?), but many will delight us. Others might leave us with questions about the way our own culture eats. Still others might offend our hosts or guests because we are unaware of their cultural rituals around a meal (Who sits where at the table? Who eats first? Which food or drink might be considered inappropriate?).

The exercise below is meant to foster a discussion about these issues. The questions are not comprehensive or meant to limit the conversation. They are intended only to offer a framework. Feel free to ask other questions and share additional thoughts as they occur to you. Let it be a conversation, rather than an assignment to complete. Above all, show respect for the cultural perspectives of others, seek information and understanding, and do not judge the mealtime rituals of one culture over and against that of another.

There are two ways to approach this exercise; choose either or both.

1. Invite someone who is from the country/region to which you are traveling and lives in or near your own hometown to be your guest at one of your team meetings. Using the questions below, ask your guest(s) to help you understand the differences in culture surrounding the mealtime that he/she/they may have experienced coming from their own culture to yours.

2. Plan a specific meal with your hosts during the mission experience to address the issues of culture and meals. While volunteers might be eating with people from the community in which they serve each day, ask the hosts to provide a meal that would fully express their traditions. (Note: It is natural to offer to pay for this meal, but be aware that part of your host's culture could be that they provide this meal themselves. Be sensitive in your negotiations.)

Use the questions below to start the discussion. Invite team members to offer their contrasts and insights when appropriate.

After the meal, reflect on what you experienced and learned from this exercise. Ask how this experience influenced your understanding in those areas raised in Phase One — theology, spiritual formation, cultural awareness, and social justice.

DISCUSSION THEMES AND QUESTIONS

Family and Guests

Who is usually present at the table for a meal?

How do persons know if they are welcome at a meal?

Are invitations formal, informal, or just understood?

What are the seating protocols?

In what special ways are guests treated?

The Conversation

Do meals start or end in prayer?

What is considered the purpose of these prayers?

Is it customary to engage in conversation while eating or does conversation follow the meal?

What is discussed at the table?

What subjects are taboo?

Who is/is not allowed to participate?

The Menu

Who decides what foods are served?

Is there a variation of food from meal to meal within one day?

What foods and drinks are forbidden?

Are guests or family allowed a choice of what they can eat and what they can refuse?

What foods are considered staples?

What foods are considered luxuries?

What comprises an "ordinary" meal that the family might eat on a regular basis?

What comprises a feast for special occasions?

How do you indicate to your hosts that you have eaten enough?

What happens to leftovers?

Dietary/Health Issues

Do some persons restrict their diet because of health issues?

Do persons reduce or increase their food intake to lose or gain weight?

Do persons choose to avoid certain foods for health or moral reasons?

Do the foods people eat or avoid eating reflect religious, cultural, or ethical issues?

Is there a required ritual to clean or wash before, during, or after a meal?

Social Issues

Do men and women interact and sit together or separately at the meal?

Are children included or excluded in any way?

Does any particular food (or absence of food) reflect the socioeconomic standing of a family?

How do you show your appreciation for the meal and the hospitality of the host(s)?

Is alcohol included or excluded from the table for any reason?

Is the use of electronics at the meal discouraged, forbidden, or allowed?

What interruptions during a meal are permitted? forbidden?

When do you know the meal is over and you are permitted to leave?

How long is it polite to stay after the meal? When have you overstayed your welcome?

ANSWERING GOD'S CALL
MEDITATION DURING THE MISSION EXPERIENCE

SCRIPTURE

The earth is the LORD's, and all that is in it, the world, and those who live in it; for he has founded it on the seas, and established it on the rivers (Ps. 24:1-2).

Declare [God's] glory among the nations, his marvelous works among all the peoples (Ps. 96:3).

"When you enter a town and are received, eat what they set before you, heal anyone who is sick, and tell them, 'God's kingdom is right on your doorstep'" (Luke 10:8-9, THE MESSAGE).

REFLECTION

Volunteers, you are here at the invitation of your hosts. Hosts, these volunteers are your guests. Together you are called to a mutual task: to touch one another's lives, to build a community of faith, to serve one another and the wider community in the name of Jesus, and to share in an experience of God's reign. This relational task is more important than any project that has been planned. You are not called to get a job done, but to incarnate the reign of God. Whatever plans you have made for this time together, your call now is to be present to what is happening. Look. Listen. Ponder.

I have been with guests who took for granted what their hosts had to offer, who made unreasonable requests, and who expressed criticism and disdain instead of appreciation. I have been with hosts who tried too hard to please, saying, "No problem" to a request and then making extreme efforts to obtain what was asked for at great cost to themselves and their community. Both behaviors breed resentment and hurt feelings.

In addition, if you are experiencing some degree of culture shock because people and events are not as you expected them to be, you may find it more difficult to see things from the viewpoint of others. Although you may feel uncomfortable, know that being outside your comfort zone will likely cause you to grow.

How would you describe the kind of host or guest you want to be? Thoughtful? Considerate? Caring? Appreciative? Generous? Kind? What would you add to this list?

What behaviors would you expect from that kind of host or guest (whichever you are)? Would you want your hosts to cause harm by trying too hard to please you? Would you want your guests to feel guilty because they do not understand the limits of your situation?

What have you observed that matches your expectations?

What is different from what you expected?

RESPONSE

When you wake in the morning, instead of thinking about what you are going to do, remind yourself to watch for what God is doing and consider how you might respond. When things do not go as planned, ask yourself what God may want you to learn from that experience.

Record in your journal each day several people, places, or events for which you are grateful and that speak to you of God's glory and creative power. Express words of appreciation to persons you encounter. List some of them here. Review the covenant you and your team developed for your time together. Record times in your journal when you have been grateful for this covenant. If you think parts of it should be changed or added to, tell your team leader or spiritual guide and ask for this to be discussed in a team meeting.

PRAYER

Lord of all creation, we delight in your world and in all that you have made. Thank you for the mystery that lies behind things as they appear on the surface, and help us to see, hear, smell, feel, and taste with gratitude and wonder. Keep us mindful of your love for all creation and your compassion for all who suffer. Make us instruments of your healing love. In Jesus' name. *Amen.*

TEAM CULTURAL ACTIVITY

Mission and Culture: Biblical Reflections

During one or more of the team's sessions, the team could invite the host leader to join them in taking another look at Luke 13. One goal of this time is to look for the parallels between the text and the mission context. Ask the host to comment on the team and its work. Are there times when the volunteers have been "bent over" or have acted like the leaders in the synagogue? Create an opportunity for the host and the team to reflect together on the implications of this text in relation to their experience together.

While in the midst of the mission experience, the team and the host, thinking again about the "bent over" woman and the synagogue leaders, might consider whether these two perspectives are present in the mission context, present in the team itself, and present in persons within the host community. Discuss ways in which clinging to long-established culturally based ways of doing things may cripple the mission context because of culturally based judgments.

=========================== TEAM ACTIVITY ===========================

Questions and Statements for Discussion and Reflection

Ask team members to identify their own "bent overness." This might include cultural ways of behaving (too much task orientation, wanting to see their solution as the only solution, and so on) that are in need of healing. Or it might be rigid attitudes about the "superior" political or economic systems of the volunteers' home country that makes it difficult for the volunteers to be respectful of the choices of host partners.

Are there places where the familiar ways and perspectives of the team members have come into conflict with the familiar ways and practices of those in the host community (both mistaken for mandates of faith)? Is there an urge to criticize or offer solutions to political realities based upon ways of doing things in the home country?

Name some personal limits that affect the ability to work in the mission context. Team members should look again at their individual lists and the collective team list on needs and wants. It may be that volunteers feel their ability to work in the mission context is limited.

Ask team members to identify attitudes like those of the synagogue leaders that may be affecting their participation.

Invite team members to create a role-play of some of these attitudes as a part of the team's time for spiritual formation.

SEARCH ME AND KNOW MY HEART
MEDITATION DURING THE MISSION EXPERIENCE

SCRIPTURE

I'm glad in God, far happier than you would ever guess—happy that you're again show-ing such strong concern for me. Not that you ever quit praying and thinking about me. You just had no chance to show it. Actually, I don't have a sense of needing anything personally. I've learned by now to be quite content whatever my circumstances. I'm just as happy with little as with much, with much as with little. I've found the recipe for being happy whether full or hungry, hands full or hands empty. Whatever I have, wherever I am, I can make it through anything in the One who makes me who I am. I don't mean that your help didn't mean a lot to me—it did. It was a beautiful thing that you came alongside me in my troubles (Phil. 4:10-14, THE MESSAGE).

But he said to me, "My grace is sufficient for you, for my power is made perfect in weak-ness." Therefore I will boast all the more gladly about my weaknesses, so that Christ's power may rest on me (2 Cor. 12:9, NIV).

Surely God is my salvation; I will trust, and will not be afraid, for the LORD GOD is my strength and my might; he has become my salvation (Isa. 12:2).

Be joyful always; pray continually; give thanks in all circumstances, for this is God's will for you in Christ Jesus (1 Thess. 5:16-18, NIV).

REFLECTION

Stop! Drop whatever you are doing and focus on what is happening inside you. Do not be afraid of the feelings that surface; receive those feelings as friends who are trying to tell you something. Marshall Rosenberg tells us that our feelings can guide us to an understanding of our needs. Needs are universal, but arise in us differently depending on our past experiences and present circumstances. Are you happy? That means you have needs that are being met: needs for connection, comfort, meaning, or peace. Are you sad? Perhaps the needs for nurturing and appreciation are at play within you. Are you lonely? Perhaps the need for companionship is calling for attention. Are you angry? Go beyond your anger to discover if there is a secondary cause, such as hurt, fear, loneliness, or the need for support.[2]

Rosenberg points out that many of us automatically assign blame when we are angry.[3] Because I grew up in a household where I learned that it is not nice to be angry, I used to look for someone to blame when I felt anger build up inside me. Fortunately, I later learned that anger is a normal defense mechanism. Anger tells us that something needs attention. I have learned that I can express my anger and whatever is behind it without attacking or diminishing another person.

All living creatures experience pleasure and pain, but what distinguishes human beings from the rest of creation is our intelligence, the ability God gave us to use our minds to explore, understand, and make decisions. As Paul eloquently writes to the church at Philippi, we can learn to be content in any circumstance by changing the way we think about it. Our thoughts, especially our judgments, may trigger uncomfortable feelings. If circumstances are not as we wish them to be, we often complain that we deserve better, that life is unfair, and that someone should make things more to our liking. Or we can talk to ourselves with empathy ("Yes, this is difficult for me") and confidence ("Although this is not what I would have chosen, with the help of God and my friends, I can handle it.")

During a construction project, I was asked to help remove debris thrown to the ground by the demolition crew. I found some empty cement bags, piled chunks of concrete on them, and hauled them to the designated spot. At first, sweating in the hot sun and wiping dust from my face, I felt demeaned by this menial and unpleasant assignment. My master's degree and teaching skills were useless here! Then I laughed at myself, decided to accept this as a lesson in humility, and cheerfully finished the task. Later that evening, my wounded ego recovered as I helped some eager students practice speaking English. I was glad I had not spoiled the afternoon by feeling sorry for myself.

Ask yourself, "What is happening within me? What am I thinking, feeling, and needing?" Welcome those thoughts with self-empathy. Be kind to yourself, as you would be to someone who expresses similar feelings to you. Consider how you might think differently about whatever is triggering your feelings.

How have I been able to use my gifts within the mission context?

Which of my vulnerabilities are in play?

RESPONSE

List here and thank God for the ways your needs are being met.

Focus on the unmet needs underlying your uncomfortable feelings and explore creative options for satisfying them, perhaps in ways you have not thought of before.

PRAYER

Lord of life, thank you for your constant presence and care. We do not ask for freedom from discomfort or worry, but pray for your spirit to grant guidance, strength, and grace that we may triumph through our trials and rest in your eternal Love. Through Jesus Christ. *Amen.*

═══ TEAM ACTIVITY ═══

1. Assessing the Cultural Baseline within the Mission Context

The team members will want to use the cultural identity list they created during the orientation as a starting point for identifying where cultural issues are coming up in their experiences with persons from the host community. The team members can create a list of things they feel they are doing well in terms of cultural awareness as well as identifying areas that need more work.

2. Assessing the Cultural Baseline: Understanding the Cultural Identity of the Volunteers

Team members will need to take time to discuss changes in their perceptions about their own cultural identity. Individual team members might share what they have learned about their national, racial, class, and ethnic identities while in the mission context. For example, a Korean American member of the team might have the following exchange within the mission context:

Volunteer: I'm pleased to meet you Mr. Kamau.

Mr. Kamau (host): Hello Mr. Lee, I am pleased to meet you. Are you Chinese or American?

Volunteer: I am Chinese American.

Mr. Kamau host: You're an American then.

Questions for discussion

What does this dialogue reveal about the attitude of the person from the host country toward people from the United States?

How do volunteers of various backgrounds feel about this attitude?

How might persons from different backgrounds respond?

How can this experience help members of the volunteer team think about ways of building relationships in the mission context?

3. Reviewing Host Perspectives (Alternative Team Activity)

Return to the list of attitudes shared by host communities about volunteers (pages 72–73). Ask team members to share examples of their own behavior. Invite them to consider if they now see anything in their own behavior reflected on the list.

For example:

> *Volunteer: When will we be able to get started putting up the interior walls?*
>
> *Mr. Patel (host): Well, there have been some delays with the materials, and I don't know exactly when we will get started.*
>
> *Volunteer: But you know, Mr. Patel, we only have one week to be here, and we really must get started on the project if we are going to finish it on time.*
>
> *Mr. Patel: I know you're anxious to meet your deadlines. I will speak again to the supplier about the delivery of the materials.*

(For additional dialogues or ideas on how to write your own, see *Cross-Cultural Dialogues: 74 Brief Encounters with Cultural Difference* by Craig Storti.)

Questions for discussion

What are the differences in perspective of the volunteer and Mr. Patel?

How does one's cultural perspective reflect his or her comments?

What might Mr. Patel be trying to convey through his response to the volunteer?

What is the volunteer's principal concern, and what alternative responses might the volunteer give?

Evaluating Comfort Spaces

There are bound to be jarring moments when entering a new context, times when everything seems difficult or foreign or frightening. These feelings are likely to arise not on the first day when everything seems new and interesting but after the team settles into its routine. It is at this time that feelings of culture shock and homesickness may begin to surface. It is neither possible nor desirable to recreate all the comfort spaces that were identified earlier, but it is important for individuals and the team to give permission to find those comfort spaces that will help them function in the mission context. It may be something as simple as access to a particular kind of music or knowing where in the community there is a clean toilet.

TEAM ACTIVITY

Discussion on Team's Current Comfort Status

The team leader asks team members to review their journal responses to the comfort spaces exercises. Identify the spaces where no problems exist that were anticipated and the places where problems exist that are impacting the mission experience and task. Identify the team's ideas about addressing these issues.

Ask team members to lift up a particular situation in the mission context where feelings of discomfort occur. If the discussion points to some common problems, the team is invited to gather in small groups to create brief dialogues of these situations and think about alternative ways they can be handled.

Revisiting Personal National Identities and Attitudes/Perspectives

Volunteers will want to revisit the picture of their individual home context they drew during the orientation (examples of the important elements of their personal national identity and their attitudes and perceptions toward the mission context and nation before their experience). Now, from the perspective of the mission context, volunteers can take advantage of the opportunity to reflect on those earlier attitudes and perspectives. They can also think about which ones were correct, which were incorrect, and which need to be adjusted.

TEAM ACTIVITY

1. Questions for discussion and reflection

What are some of the surprising things you learned about the host country that differ from what you imagined before you arrived?

What similarities do you notice between the host country and your own country that you did not expect?

Which of your attitudes about the host country need to be corrected?

What are some of your new understandings of the political and economic realities of the host country that may confirm or change your views before you arrived?

(For additional reflection and insights, see Phase Two, Spiritual Transformation, "Daily Reflection and Group Processing During a Mission Experience" (pages 90–91) and "Meditation During the Mission Experience: Answering God's Call" (pages 97–99).

2. Critical Analysis and Problem Solving

To goal of this activity is for team members to look at possible real-life situations through the lens of multiple perspectives and for them to search and know themselves better. They will explore how different identities affect the ways in which a volunteer perceives and reacts to these realities.

To meet the challenge of answering God's call, how do actions in the mission context affect the volunteer in host relationships both in the short-term and long-term? What other factors are at play?

To assess the actions so volunteers will be known as Christians by their love, what is the meaning of working for justice in complicated social and political situations?

Volunteer Tanya: We are invited to a dinner at the church tonight. I am really worried. They seem to eat so much meat here, and I am trying to be a vegetarian. I think I will just say I am sick and stay back.

Volunteer Mike: If you stay back it will be a big insult to the women at the church who went to a lot of trouble to prepare the food.

Volunteer Jane: Have you seen that church? It barely has a roof, and it has a dirt floor. I've never seen a water faucet there. Who knows what kind of germs may be there? I always take my hand sanitizer everywhere, and I can bring along my own water.

Team Leader: How do you think the members of the church will react if some of us don't go, and the rest of us seem afraid to eat the food?

The object of this exercise is not to judge the behaviors of individuals but to discover ways in which a team can work together to deal with difficult situations so that participants increase understanding of themselves and of the mission context.

The Process

A written scenario of events is presented in the mission context (perhaps during the preparation time for returning home). Team members read the scenario and create an improvised role-play of the basic events of the scenario, supplementing it from their own experience. Allow about ten minutes for this exercise.

Invite the team to form three groups to discuss and analyze each scenario from the starting point of three basic perspectives:

- Answering God's call—perspectives on mission relationships
- Search me and know my heart—cultural assumptions such as comfort spaces, class, and race identity
- Know I am a Christian by my love—justice issues, power dynamics

Note: Theological perspectives should both underlie and be part of the discussion on each of these three perspectives. The discussions are not exclusive; they should involve the interaction of insights from all three perspectives. Groups should summarize their discussion with at least one and as many as three key insights and share them with the entire team. The purpose of the group discussion is to share insights on the three perspectives, develop ideas for alternative approaches when an approach failed within the actual mission context, and conclude with a summary of lessons learned.

Possible Real-life Mission Scenarios
Scene 1: This scene takes place at a small Methodist church construction site in a Latin American country. It addresses the fundamental question of "Who is in charge?"

One US team member is a retired engineer (RE) and the construction leader for the team. The RE communicates with the local construction leader (LCL) then guides the rest of the team in construction. Early on, the RE begins to show his authority, and he is somewhat overbearing with the LCL who tries to explain how to build a wall that will eventually become part of the church. The LCL finally gives up and lets the RE do it his way. Three days later it is obvious to everyone that the wall is crooked. The LCL instructs the team to tear the wall down, much to the embarrassment of the team and the RE who apologizes profusely. The RE reassures the LCL that although time has been lost, he has already contacted his home church, and it has agreed to raise the additional funds to replace the materials used in the crooked wall.

Scene 2: This scene takes place in a Latin American town with no hotels. Team members stay in homes of local church members. It addresses the issues of language barriers, privilege, entitlement, and pre-planning.

Team members stay in the homes of local church members since there are no hotels in the small town. There are two team members per home. After the first night, one team member complains that the hostess is not very friendly, does not speak English, did not give directions on how to use the shower, and did not offer coffee that morning. The team leader from the United States talks with the local team leader (who sympathizes with the situation because of her own experience in the United States with her hostesses who could not speak much Spanish) and arranges to switch the US team member to another home with a fellow Spanish-speaking team member.

Scene 3: This scene takes place in a large urban area in the northeastern United States. It addresses the issues of racial identity and justice. Focus should be on the racial identities of *all* team members.

As team leader, you have prepared your team to go to South Africa. As a part of the orientation, you invite a person from South Africa to share her experience of *apartheid* (understood "apart-hate") and how racial divisions continue to impact her country. The team has been taught that the words *black*, *colored*, and *white* are commonly used as descriptions for people of different ethnicities, and that the struggle with racial prejudice and racial profiling continues, even as many positive changes occur in South Africa. Your team is made up of persons with a variety of racial identities, but it is predominantly Caucasian. In one of your evening gathering times, an African American member of your team expresses hurt and anger toward the white members of the team for their apparent ease and acceptance of "the way things are there." White members of the team defend their attitudes by saying that they care about what happens, but it is not their country and they have no right to interfere.

Scene 4: A UMVIM team is working alongside an indigenous group of people on a mission construction project in Guatemala. The indigenous group is comprised of Methodists. This scene addresses the issues of power dynamics and justice, social and cultural perspectives, the meanings of solidarity, and the realities of reconciliation.

You have given your team some background information during orientation about the significant in-country tension between the military police and the indigenous people. While working on a building, several military police arrive on the site and ask that the team join them for a required gathering of the village. Some of your team members object and want to stay on the site. Your Methodist hosts are quiet but say they think the whole group should go. Ecumenical church leaders who have been in conversation with leaders from opposing political sides about the possibilities for reconciliation are also in the country. Church leaders suggest an ecumenical service to be attended both by indigenous leaders and by members of the military. The ecumenical leaders from other countries are anxious to see the success of their visit, and they urge the local indigenous leadership to attend the event along with the visiting leaders and the mission volunteer team. The local leadership agrees to attend, but they privately express their pain at having to attend a worship service with the military leaders who have caused their community so much suffering.

Scene 5: A church decides to conduct a mission trip within its home state and/or country this year. This scene addresses the issues of privilege, class, and awareness related to participating in a mission context within one's own state and/or country.

Your church's mission leadership works with the conference mission office to organize a mission to work on a fellowship hall for one of the national mission institutions. Some of the team members participate in your orientation meetings and some do not. Those who do not say they have visited the national mission institution many times before. Besides, it is in their own state (or country), and they already know everything they need to know in order to work there. During the session, some participants use their cell phones to send text messages while the representative of the mission institution is speaking. During the question-and-answer period, questions reveal certain prejudices and historical issues from the mission institution's relationship to the conference, such as support through conference appropriations and scholarships set aside for students of the mission institution.

THEY WILL KNOW WE ARE CHRISTIANS BY OUR LOVE
MEDITATION DURING THE MISSION EXPERIENCE

SCRIPTURE

Jesus replied: "'Love the Lord your God with all your heart and with all your soul and with all your mind.' This is the first and greatest commandment. And the second is like it: 'Love your neighbor as yourself'" (Matt. 22:37-39, NIV).

Have we not all one father? Has not one God created us? (Mal. 2:10).

So then you are no longer strangers and aliens, but you are citizens with the saints and also members of the household of God (Eph. 2:19).

Therefore encourage one another and build each other up, just as in fact you are doing. Now we ask you, brothers [and sisters], to acknowledge those who work hard among you, who care for you in the Lord and who admonish you. Hold them in the highest regard in love because of their work. Live in peace with each other. And we urge you, brothers [and sisters], warn those who are idle, encourage the timid, help the weak, be patient with everyone. Make sure that nobody pays back wrong for wrong, but always try to be kind to each other and to everyone else (1 Thess. 5:11-15, NIV).

My dear brothers [and sisters], take note of this: Everyone should be quick to listen, slow to speak and slow to become angry, for [human] anger does not bring about the righteous life that God desires (Jas. 1:19-20, NIV).

We love because he first loved us. If anyone says, "I love God," yet hates his brother, he is a liar. For anyone who does not love his brother, whom he has seen, cannot love God, whom he has not seen. And he has given us this command: Whoever loves God must also love his brother (1 John 4:19-21, NIV).

REFLECTION

Christian love means making a decision to put the concerns and needs of another person or persons at the top of our priority list. Perhaps it is essential to love ourselves that way as well, considering Jesus' wording of the second greatest commandment, "Love your neighbor as yourself" (Matt. 22:39). Yes, we are encouraged to look beyond our own needs, and the Gospel of John states clearly that there is no greater love than "to lay down one's life for one's friends" (John 15:13). Paul, however, advises the church in Corinth to "let all that you do be done in love" (1 Cor. 16:14). This suggests to me that if we feel resentful or guilty because we are neglecting our own health, safety, and well-being, as well as that of our family, we may need to rethink some of our choices. If we are unkind to ourselves, harshly self-critical, and obsessively perfectionistic, we are likely to treat others the same way. Maybe self-care is not a matter of selfishness, but a matter of good stewardship.

We may admire those who seem to act without thought for their own well-being; but if they then expect us to repay them with unquestioning loyalty and boundless appreciation, we might rightfully feel manipulated. Those who act out of true generosity and an apparent overflow of love inspire others to give more freely. Consider, for example, parents who abundantly provide their children with a blend of unconditional love and firm guidance. Their children will likely grow up to be more appreciative, considerate, and generous than those raised in a neglectful or hostile environment. Regardless of my experiences in the past, how do I care for myself now so I can more freely and generously love others?

I was disappointed and upset with a friend who did not attend my mother's memorial service, although I understood the reasons why she could not come. Instead of berating myself for my feelings, I thought long and hard about what I really needed. Finally, I realized that I wanted her to know my mother as she was remembered in that service and that connecting with her was more valuable to me than making her feel bad about not coming. I chose another occasion to show her pictures and share some stories of my mother. My hurt and disappointment evaporated in a time of sharing that

I would have missed completely had I not taken time to listen to my heart and discern the need underlying my feelings.

Think of someone who seems to function out of an overflow of love. Why do you think he or she is able to act this way? What would it take for you to be able to act like that? Think of the persons with whom you are sharing this mission experience and consider what needs of theirs you might be able to meet.

RESPONSE

When you are aware of a need that has arisen in you, consider various options for meeting that need. If you decide to make a request of someone, use an "I message" and be sure it does not sound like a demand. Before you speak, be clear about what you want to accomplish. If you are tempted by a desire to prove the other person wrong, rethink your purpose and seek to connect instead.

As you interact with others during this mission experience, do not take what they say personally or focus on your response to them. Seek instead to understand the underlying needs that influence their words and actions. Respond with empathy, even if you disagree with what they say or cannot provide what they need.

PRAYER

Divine love, so fill my heart that I may respond to others with kindness, caring, and empathy. Keep me mindful that not everything that happens is about me, and remind me of my freedom to choose my response in any given situation. In the name of the Christ. *Amen.*

TEAM CULTURAL AND JUSTICE ACTIVITIES

Continuing Relationships with the Mission Context

Following a positive mission experience, team members are always anxious to consider the possibilities for ongoing relationships with the mission context. Ongoing relationships can take the form of future assistance through fund-raising, volunteer opportunities, and advocacy at home. An important part of this conversation needs to be thinking through the cultural awareness implications of any future plans.

> How can your ministry have a long-term impact? See Appendix for "In Mission Together: 50/50 Partnership Covenant."

Volunteers can use the cultural identity information created in their journals as one tool to evaluate proposals for ongoing relationships from a cultural awareness perspective. Enthusiasm for work in the mission context will probably be high. Team members will want to look at their list of desired outcomes and relate it to the list that the hosts shared of undesirable volunteer behavior. For example, team members need to ask themselves whether the "missionary mentality" (the feeling that volunteers can solve every problem in the mission context) is resurfacing.

Volunteer Jane: We know that they need vacation Bible school materials. We have a lot of materials in our church. We could send them some of our materials.

Volunteer Mary: One of the things I learned was that when I tried to tell some of the stories from our materials, the children didn't understand what I was talking about because many of them had never seen a television or knew anybody who actually owned a car. The stories are good, but they are for children in our community.

Volunteer Susan: You are right. I have an idea. Ms. Gomez is a good teacher, so maybe I can show her our materials and we can work together to see how some of our stories might be adapted for the children here.

Volunteer Randy: That's a good idea! And maybe some of the materials they use here we could take back to our churches to help children in our community learn from the children here.

Identifying Justice Issues

Now that the team has spent time in the mission context they will be better equipped to comment on justice issues within it. The discussion below can help the team share and sharpen their perceptions about what is happening in the mission context as well as add complexity to their understanding of the work for justice. For a deeper understanding, the team should refer to the article, "Christian Mission in a Time of Globalization: Doing Justice outside the Gate!" found in Phase One of this handbook (pages 23–38).

=== **TEAM ACTIVITY** ===

Questions for Discussion

What signs of justice/injustice did you observe today? Who is "outside the gates?"

What was being done?

What role, if any, did you think the church should play?

How does the reality of the mission context compare to the justice issues you named during the orientation?

What new insights does your team have about justice as a result of your experience in the mission context?

Preparing to Return Home

Before leaving the mission context, the volunteer team must begin to think about what will happen when they return home. Cultural awareness is a critical part of this thinking. The advantage of starting the conversation in the mission context is that it can be a conversation with all members of the team present, and the mission host can also participate. Volunteers and hosts can think together about ongoing relationships with the mission context and what might be done at home. This conversation provides an opportunity for everyone who has been involved in the mission experience to find ways to build and share that special time and to think about the future together.

Volunteers are likely to be anxious about how those at home will respond when they share their mission experiences. They may wonder if everyone is excited to hear about the mission experience or if their patience for listening will run out after five or ten minutes. They may also ask themselves, "How will we use our new cultural, national, spiritual, and theological understandings and function differently in our home context?"

TEAM ACTIVITY

1. New Understandings and Opportunities

In one team session near the end of the time in the mission context, the team leader might ask team members to think about places in their lives where they see themselves functioning differently because of their experience. Direct team members to think of what they would like to happen when they return home, opportunities that might open for them, and obstacles they may encounter.

Volunteers might want to consider a situation in which the question is raised, "Why can we not just take up a collection and send them some money?" This question presents an opportunity for volunteers. They are now prepared to answer this question by discussing the various options for assistance in light of their new cultural awareness and understanding of the mission context.

2. Staying Connected: Building a Support System

The team can begin to think about how they will stay connected and provide support and encouragement to one another around their new cultural awareness insights. One of the difficult parts of returning from a meaningful mission experience is readjusting to home. Going from a society where resources are scarce and people use and re-use everything in order to survive can create a difficult return to a society where things are thrown away long before their life is over. It is possible for a volunteer to feel disoriented in his or her own society. A volunteer may experience a kind of reverse culture shock. Under these situations, the ability to talk and share feelings with other volunteers is important for learning how to live with a new cultural awareness.

The team should spend a session brainstorming ideas about the advantages and disadvantages of staying connected to one another after their time in the mission context. Discuss what they might want to achieve by staying connected—spiritual reflection, strategic thinking, problem solving, sharing new insights, action planning, and the like. Explore potential means for continuing contact with one another, including buddy systems. Conclude with individuals volunteering to take responsibility for specific types of communication and leadership in relation to staying connected.

Closing Reflections
Near the end of the mission experience, you will want to hold a time of group reflection on the entire event. Hosts and volunteers can meet separately or together depending on what the team leaders and spiritual guides think best. You might use the following questions, as well as some of the suggestions in "Engaging in Group Conversation" (pages 49–51).

Choose one word to describe your experience.

Share one of your most memorable moments.

If you were going to take one photograph or paint one picture, who or what would be in it?

What was your most positive experience?

What was most challenging?

Who made a positive impact on your life?

Which worship moment or devotion stands out for you?

When did you feel God calling you to do something specific?

When did you feel God empowering you to do something difficult?

What have you learned about the privileges you enjoy because of where you live, your cultural context, economic factors, and the color of your skin?

What do you think will be hardest for you to explain to someone who was not involved in your mission experience?

What will you want others to know about your experience?

What changes do you anticipate in the way you will live after this experience?

For questions related to justice issues, see "Team Justice Activity: Identifying Justice Issues" (page 117).

Closing Worship

The final worship service of an UMVIM mission experience often includes Communion, as participants gather to remember the last supper Jesus ate with his disciples and his use of an ordinary loaf of bread and a cup of wine to symbolize his continuing presence in their lives, even after his death. The breaking of the loaf and pouring out of the wine remind us of his servanthood, suffering, and sacrifice for all God's children. Closing services may be formal (as when we invited an entire Russian farming village to share with us in a Communion ritual) or informal (a dozen mission volunteers sharing grape juice and bread in the cargo plane returning them to the United States after a mission experience in Haiti). Team leaders should see to it that everyone gets to participate in shared rituals, parting prayers, group hugs, or whatever is needed to bring closure to the experience and celebrate what it has meant to the volunteers involved.

Preparing to Return Home

Team leaders and spiritual guides should prepare their team members for what they may experience when they return home. This conversation is most effective if held with the volunteers and hosts separately prior to departure. Participants often feel so elated by their experiences that they cannot wait to tell others about them. Sometimes they are disappointed when those back home do not seem to appreciate or fully understand what they are hearing. Encourage team members to tell others as much as they seem willing to hear, but to call other team members or those who have been involved in previous mission experiences when they want to relive the wonder and excitement of this special time.[4]

Prepare volunteers for the probability that they will experience some depression when the adrenaline of the experience wears off and exhaustion kicks in. Encourage them to practice self-empathy during the stress of reentry into their lives back home. Emphasize the importance of taking care of one's physical needs by resting and healthy eating and one's emotional needs through spiritual centering, journaling, and spending quiet time in their homes and with family and friends.[5]

Team members may also feel guilty when they experience relief and joy that the mission experience is over, especially if they return to more affluent and comfortable surroundings. They may deny the impact of the experience and try to act as if nothing has changed, particularly if they do not have the opportunity to talk with persons who understand what they have been through or if they do not see how to respond to what feels like a new claim on their lives.[6]

You might conclude this time of preparation for returning home by inviting team members to write letters to themselves that you will mail to them in six months. Distribute paper and envelopes for volunteers to address to themselves and in which they can seal their letters before giving them to you. You might also distribute a simple written evaluation form on which they can note what they thought went well, what they thought could have been better, and what they would like team leaders to consider for future mission experiences.

Be sure to set a reunion date, preferably within the next month or so, and suggest that team members use one or more of the meditations for AFTER the mission experience (pages 127, 131, and 135) before the occasion. If some team members live a long distance from the others, consider ways to keep them connected, perhaps by setting up a private group on a social media site or by scheduling a conference call.

AFTER

THE MISSION EXPERIENCE

INTRODUCTION

The task of growth and transformation continues when the volunteer team returns to its home context. The days and months following the mission experience provide an opportunity for volunteers to integrate all they have learned, reflect on what it means to *answer God's call*, deepen their understanding of how to *search and know the heart*, and help so that *others will know they are Christians by their love*. It is an opportunity for the hosts and the team leader to assess the experience and identify learnings for future mission experiences. Each participant in the mission experience will need to assess many different aspects of their learning as a result of the experience. This includes everything from a new respect for diversity of cultural and political perspectives of others to personal changes in individual comfort spaces. The team should solidify ongoing support and communication among team members. Finally, team members can look again at their growing understanding of the relationship of the mission task to the cultural identities defined at the beginning of the mission experience.

ANSWERING GOD'S CALL
MEDITATION AFTER THE MISSION EXPERIENCE

SCRIPTURE

Is not this the kind of fasting that I choose: to loose the bonds of injustice, to undo the thongs of the yoke, to let the oppressed go free and to break every yoke? Is it not to share your food with the hungry, and bring the homeless poor into your house; when you see the naked, to cover them, and not to hide yourself from your own kin? Then your light shall break forth like the dawn, and your healing shall spring up quickly; your vindicator shall go before you, and the glory of the LORD will be your rear guard. Then you shall call, and the LORD will answer; you shall cry for help, and he will say, Here I am. If you remove the yoke from among you, the pointing of the finger, the speaking of evil, if you offer your food to the hungry, and satisfy the needs of the afflicted, then your light shall rise in the darkness and your gloom be like the noonday (Isa. 58:6-10).

REFLECTION

Home again. A mixture of emotions floods over us. We experience relief and joy as we reunite with those most dear to us, savoring again the comforts of our own homes. We also feel sadness and longing for what we have left behind: new friends, the unique beauty of a different place, a daily rhythm of prayer and worship, the opportunity to focus on living the gospel each day, the experience of supportive community, the deep sense of spiritual connection and dependence on God. The questions haunt us—What do we do with our new insights and understandings? What is God calling us to do now and in the days, weeks, months, and years ahead?

N. T. Wright, in his recent book *How God Became King: The Forgotten Story of the Gospels,* claims that the church is mistaken when it emphasizes "rescuing" people from the world, a concept that stems from the Middle Ages and misses the point of the Gospels. "The gospels," he says, "are there waiting to inform a new generation for holistic mission, to embody, to explain, and advocate new ways of ordering communities, nations, and the world. The church belongs at the very heart of the world, to be the place of prayer and holiness at the point where the world is in pain—not to be a somewhat 'religious' version of the world, on the one hand, or a detached, heavenly minded enclave, on the other."[1] According to Wright, the Gospels promise that the world, even with everything that is wrong with it, will be put right "through the Spirit-led work of Jesus' followers," who will "reflect God's wise ordering of the world and so shine light into its dark corners, bringing judgment and mercy where it is badly needed."[2] Joseph Mathews, founder and guru of the Ecumenical Institute in the Chicago area in the 1950s and 1960s, also sought to recapture the spirit of early Christians, describing them as "a body of people who moved out into the twilight zone, into the no-man's land onto the beachhead between the No Longer and the Not Yet. They were calling into question the structures of humanness and their inadequacies and dreaming new visions of more adequate structures that would minister unto the well-being of all. They laid down their lives to bring these structures into being for the sake of the mass of humanity."[3] Mathews inspired many people to think of themselves as "Perpetual Revolutionaries" working for a better world "as long as one person is suffering."[4]

Where do you see injustice and suffering at home? Who is outside the gates in your community? Who is outside the gates in the world at large?

The slogan "Think globally; act locally" has become a popular way to challenge the decisions and actions of individuals, corporations, communities, and governments. What does this slogan prompt you to consider doing differently in your personal life and in the life of the communities of which you are a part?

RESPONSE

Carefully plan how you will tell the story of what you have experienced and learned. Know that persons who did not share in your mission experience or who have not participated in something similar may have difficulty understanding the impact your experience has had on you. Choose several interesting stories to share that might hold the interest of others and that illustrate the points you want to make—the difficult challenges that some people face and what you understand to be the causes, the deep faith and spirituality of those with whom you shared the experience, the simple delight of focusing entirely on the mission without the distractions and concerns of your normal life.

Invite others to join you in following up on your mission experience by supporting causes that will benefit persons in need or by reading books or watching movies that will deepen your understanding of the people you met, their strengths, and their challenges. Invite others to join with you in learning more about those who suffer injustice in your own community and finding ways to act on their behalf and to be in ministry with them.

PRAYER

Creator God, we thank you for all the blessings and the challenges of our mission experience, and we thank you for our safe return home. While part of us still wanders, caught up in memories of those we met and of the adventures we shared, help us savor those memories and new insights even as we try to catch up with things undone and with those who have awaited our return. Above all, help us hear your call to do your will so that your kingdom may come "on earth as it is in heaven." May we respond with love and gratitude for all you have already done and for the promise of your unending love. In Jesus' name. *Amen.*

TEAM ACTIVITY

Collective spiritual reflections on Luke 13

Either in person or through electronic communication, team members can engage in a final reflection on the story of the bent over woman in Luke 13 in order to think once again about the cultural identity/awareness implications of their mission experience. Invite team members to share their responses to the questions on the next page.

Reread Luke 13:10-17. Identify the five ways in which Jesus acts in this text: teaching, seeing, laying on of hands, chastising, invoking justice.

Consider your recent mission experience. How many of these actions did you see within your mission context?

Name those who were involved in these actions—volunteers, hosts, mutual activities between volunteers and hosts.

How were the realities of the mission context different from that of Jesus and the bent over woman?

What could Jesus do that a volunteer might not be able to do? How did awareness of the cultural identity in the mission context affect the possibility of action?

What could a volunteer have done that was not done?

Name some opportunities for invoking justice that could be done or might be more appropriate in the home context (it might not be appropriate in the host context from the perspective of cultural awareness).

Encourage team members to write reflections as prayers or spiritual meditations and share them with one another.

SEARCH ME AND KNOW MY HEART
MEDITATION AFTER THE MISSION EXPERIENCE

SCRIPTURE

Blessed are those who trust in the LORD, whose trust is the LORD. They shall be like a tree planted by water, sending out its roots by the stream. It shall not fear when heat comes, and its leaves shall stay green; in the year of drought it is not anxious, and it does not cease to bear fruit (Jer. 17: 7-8).

Do not worry about anything, but in everything by prayer and supplication with thanksgiving let your requests be made known to God (Phil. 4:6).

And can any of you by worrying add a single hour to your span of life? . . . But strive first for the kingdom of God and his righteousness, and all these things will be given to you as well (Matt. 6:27, 33).

Create in me a clean heart, O God, and put a new and right spirit within me (Ps. 51:10).

Those who hope in the LORD will renew their strength. They will soar on wings like eagles; they will run and not grow weary, they will walk and not be faint (Isa. 40:31, NIV).

REFLECTION

The chief executive officer of an inner-city YMCA traveled to India as part of a cooperative venture with YMCAs in that country. In a conversation about the experience he commented, "I went to India with a point of view; I returned with a perspective." Exposure to another culture can challenge our beliefs about the way the world is and should be, causing us to see things in a new and different way.[5] What new perspective, insights, and awareness have you gained from your mission experience?

Spiritual disciplines that were easy to practice during your mission experience may disappear quickly as you resume your usual routines and busy schedule. It usually takes about four weeks of consecutive daily practice to establish a new habit and for that habit to become somewhat automatic. Newly acquired habits can transform attitudes and behaviors, as illustrated by the story of Cami Walker, who was diagnosed with multiple sclerosis at the age of thirty-three. While she was struggling against her physical and emotional deterioration, Cami was given an unusual prescription by a friend who had trained as an African medicine woman. Cami was told to give away twenty-nine gifts, one on each of twenty-nine consecutive days. The gifts could be tangible or intangible, but she was to bless each one. The African medicine woman also instructed Cami to make affirmations of abundance, to journal about the gifts and her experiences, and, at least once, to give away something she thought she really needed. Cami's book, *29 Gifts: How a Month of Giving Can Change Your Life,* chronicles her journey from skepticism to full-fledged commitment.[6] Cami learned to focus on what she has to offer the world instead of what she lacks and to make meaningful connections with other people. Her attitude, her health, her relationships, and her family's finances were transformed, and she founded a movement. You can learn more about this movement at www.29giftsbook.com.

RESPONSE

Decide on a new spiritual discipline to practice for the next month. You might commit to a regular time of meditation or prayer. You might fast from something that disrupts your connection to God—eating unhealthy foods, viewing uninspiring television programs, or spending time on unnecessary tasks. You might take on a practice that benefits others like that prescribed for Cami, perhaps writing letters of appreciation or performing acts of service. Whatever you decide, record your plan and progress in a journal. If you miss a day, start over again from day one in order to establish a firm habit that will last beyond your initial commitment. Note in your journal how you feel throughout the experience, what you learn from it, and how it impacts you and your relationships.

Learn more about meditation by attending workshops or by reading books, such as Jon Kabat-Zinn's *Wherever You Go, There You Are: Mindfulness Meditation in Everyday*

Life. In this book, Kabat-Zinn describes the freedom we gain when we pause long enough to experience the present moment, accept its truth, learn from it, and move on.[7] Follow the spiritual guidance of Thomas Merton, who advised, "No matter how distracted you may be, pray by peaceful, even inarticulate, efforts to center your heart upon God, who is present to you in spite of all that may be going through your mind."[8]

PRAYER

Lord Jesus, I want to be more like you. Show me the way to "see thee more clearly, love thee more dearly, follow thee more nearly, day by day."[9] *Amen.*

═══ TEAM ACTIVITY ═══

1. Cultural Identity Journaling

Start a new entry in the cultural identity pages of your journal keeping a record of experiences during the first month of return when new kinds of learning—cultural, political, economic, and spiritual—become apparent and earlier attitudes are brought into sharp relief. Reflect on the elements of a personal "cultural yardstick," thinking particularly about the areas of change that were noted during the mission experience. Incorporate naming and celebrating these areas of growth and transformation into your spiritual practice.

2. Volunteer Journal Entry

Since coming back from Malawi, I am more conscious of the amount of food we waste. In Africa, I had dinner with a family of six, and we shared two small pieces of meat along with our vegetables and *nsima* (stiff porridge). I was embarrassed because, as the visitor, they gave me the largest portion. Here at home we have three times as much food, and my little brother and sister often eat only part of what they are given and my mother throws the rest away. I cannot imagine how to make things different or what to say to them.

3. Taking Another Look at Comfort Spaces

Look at the list of comfort spaces identified BEFORE and DURING the mission experience. Think about what changes and transformations have been possible around the issue of food, language, time, and the like.

Think of ways to celebrate and communicate change in the home context.

Name, recognize, and develop strategies to accept what is necessary for the volunteer and do not represent obstacles to good mission practice.

THEY WILL KNOW WE ARE CHRISTIANS BY OUR LOVE
MEDITATION AFTER THE MISSION EXPERIENCE

SCRIPTURE

"Then those 'sheep' are going to say, 'Master, what are you talking about? When did we ever see you hungry and feed you, thirsty and give you a drink? And when did we ever see you sick or in prison and come to you? Then the King will say, 'I'm telling the solemn truth: Whenever you did one of these things to someone overlooked or ignored, that was me—you did it to me'" (Matt. 25:37-40, THE MESSAGE).

Everyone was filled with awe, and many wonders and miraculous signs were done by the apostles. All the believers were together and had everything in common. Selling their possessions and goods, they gave to anyone as he [or she] had need (Acts 2:43-45, NIV).

Keep your eyes open, hold tight to your convictions, give it all you've got, be resolute, and love without stopping (1 Cor. 16:13-14, THE MESSAGE).

But [God's] already made it plain how to live, what to do, what GOD is looking for in men and women. It's quite simple: Do what is fair and just to your neighbor, be compassionate and loyal in your love, And don't take yourself too seriously—take God seriously (Mic. 6:8, THE MESSAGE).

REFLECTION

A story circulating on the Internet tells of an anthropologist who proposed a game to children in an African tribe. He placed a basket of fruit in front of them and said that when he told them to start, they were to run toward the basket. Whoever got there first would win the fruit. When he gave them the signal to start, they all held hands and ran together, then sat down together to share the treats. The anthropologist asked them why they had run together instead of letting the fastest runner win the prize. They responded, "*Ubuntu*, how can one of us be happy if all the other ones are sad?"

Ubuntu, a word from the Xhosa culture in Africa, means, "I am because we are." In his book *No Future Without Forgiveness*, Archbishop Desmond Tutu elaborates on this idea: "A person with *Ubuntu* is open and available to others, affirming of others, does not feel threatened that others are able and good, based from a proper self-assurance that comes from knowing that he or she belongs in a greater whole and is diminished when others are humiliated or diminished, when others are tortured or oppressed."[10]

It seems to me that *Ubuntu* people would naturally be drawn to missional churches, rather than consumer churches. In churches shaped by a consumer mentality, people come to be fed, to have their needs met, and to support professionals who perform the tasks of ministry and mission. "The missional church," according to Chad Hall, "is rooted in not just the New Testament church of Acts, but in the mission of Jesus himself. A missional church lives out the church's three-dimensional calling: to be upwardly focused on God in worship that is passionate; to be inwardly focused on community among believers that is demonstrated in relationships of love and compassion; and to be outwardly focused on a world that does not yet know God."[11] Or, as Alan and Debra Hirsch state in their book *Untamed: Reactivating a Missional Form of Discipleship*, "The gospel cannot be limited to being about my personal healing and wholeness, but rather extends in and through my salvation to the salvation of the world."[12]

It is critical, even as we encourage in our churches the movement that Hall describes above, not to abuse or alienate those who may resist this change. Unfortunately, those who return from mission experiences sometimes attack the church that nurtured them and made the experience possible. It is better for us to be grateful for the faithful service of those who have given us both a heritage on which we can build and faith communities we can encourage to more effectively share Christ's love in a broken world.

RESPONSE

When you have opportunities to tell persons about your mission experience, express gratitude to the church that made the experience possible. Offer concrete ways for persons or groups to participate in ongoing ministry with those with whom you served and in other ministries that meet human needs and empower persons to live more fully.

Learn more about the barriers that leave some persons outside the gates, systems that perpetuate injustice, and strategies for restorative justice. Read books and magazines that explore these issues. Lisa Shirch's *The Little Book of Strategic Peacebuilding: A vision and framework for peace with justice,* clarifies how the "structural violence" of systems and institutions meets the needs of some people at the expense of others, causing "secondary violence": self-destructive behaviors as well as activities destructive to communities, nations, and the world.[13] Consider what is in your sphere of influence and how you can effectively work for restorative justice and peace. Invite others to participate in this learning with you. Resist the temptation to engage in blaming and name-calling. Work to build bridges between conflicted and traumatized parties, helping them find common ground on which to stand while mutually seeking satisfactory solutions to their problems and concerns. Read about the work of South Africa's Truth and Reconciliation Commission, which serves as a model for healing in Argentina, Ireland, and Israel/Palestine.[14] See pages 171–173 for additional recommended resources.

In all your relationships, seek to examine and take responsibility for your own attitudes and behaviors, showing compassion for yourself and others. Participate with your whole heart in God's mission to bring all into unity, harmony, goodness, peace, and justice.

PRAYER

Eternal God of creation, we thank you for all that has brought us to this time and place. Keep us open to your guidance and power, that we may partner with you in healing and renewing your creation, that our world might draw ever closer to your intention "that all may be one." *Amen.*

Assessing Cultural Awareness Learning

Team Leader and Host

The team leader and host might wish to exchange lists of cultural attitudes and behaviors or good and bad practices at the end of the mission experience. This is similar to those exchanged at the beginning of the mission experience. This makes it possible for both the host and the team leader to identify areas of growth and areas that will need more concentrated effort during future mission trips. It also identifies new areas for collaboration during future volunteer team experiences. The team leader can share these insights with team members and ask for their input and reflection.

Team Members

After returning home, volunteers can continue the evaluation of their own growth and cultural awareness during the mission experience. Since this work began DURING the mission context, it is a good idea to wait a month or so before taking another look at their individual learnings yardsticks.

Ongoing Communication for Support and Action

Team members should put their strategies for ongoing communication and support with one another, including sharing of ongoing insights about changes in cultural awareness, into action. Team members will recall their discussion in the mission context about obstacles that might be faced at home. For example, reverse culture shock in the home environment is a common experience for volunteers. Prior to the mission experience the volunteer may have been insensitive to disparaging attitudes toward the mission context. Upon return, however, the volunteer's listening skills are sharpened, and he or she recognizes the unfairness of these remarks.

Communication Strategies for Team Members

Use the communication system with other team members as a sounding board for new cultural insights. Share strategy ideas about potential social justice/political opportunities in the home context as a result of new cultural awareness in the mission context. Consult with one another and share experiences about attempts at public reporting on the mission experience, new cultural awareness and identity insights, as well as responses of audiences. Offer suggestions for future action.

NOTES AND SOURCES

Phase One: Setting the Context for Volunteer Mission Experiences

1. See Anthony J. Gittins, *Called to Be Sent: Co-missioned as Disciples Today* (Liguori, MO: Liguori Publications, 2008).

2. Elizabeth O'Connor, *Journey Inward, Journey Outward* (New York, NY: HarperCollins, 1975).

3. Peter J. Storey in a lecture given in Dayton, Ohio, 1997.

4. See Christopher J. H. Wright, *The Mission of God: Unlocking the Bible's Grand Narrative* (Downers Grove, IL: IVP Academic, 2006).

5. Galloway United Methodist Church; www.gallowayumc.org (accessed January 5, 2013).

6. This is the essence of a conversation with a VIM team from Oklahoma that was working in a remote area in South Africa. Many other VIM teams can witness to similar words being expressed.

7. Reverend Brenda McNeese, Director of the South Carolina Christian Action Council, quoted in the April 2011 edition of the *South Carolina United Methodist Advocate*.

8. David A. Livermore, *Serving with Eyes Wide Open: Doing Short-Term Missions with Cultural Intelligence* (Grand Rapids MI: Baker Books, 2006).

9. Tim Dearborn, *Short-Term Missions Workbook: From Mission Tourists to Global Citizens* (Downers Grove, IL: InterVarsity Press, 2003).

10. *The Book of Discipline of the United Methodist Church—2012*, (Nashville, TN: The United Methodist Publishing House, 2012), 91, ¶120.

11. Rueben P. Job, *A Guide to Retreat for All God's Shepherds* (Nashville, TN: Abingdon, 1994), 12.

12. Bill Cumming, "What Every Person Can Do" (Bath, ME: The Boothby Institute, 2012), 21.

13. David Livingstone, *Dr. David Livingstone's Cambridge Lectures*, edited by William Monk (New York, NY: Cambridge University Press, 2009).

14. Speech delivered at Riverside Church, New York, April 4, 1967.

15. Ibid.

Additional Sources

Steve Corbett and Brian Fikkert, *When Helping Hurts: How to Alleviate Poverty without Hurting the Poor . . . and Yourself* (Chicago, IL: Moody Publishers, 2009).

Eric H. F. Law, *The Wolf Shall Dwell with the Lamb: A Spirituality for Leadership in a Multicultural Community* (St. Louis, MO: Chalice Press, 1993).

Craig Storti, *Cross-Cultural Dialogues: 74 Brief Encounters with Cultural Difference* (Boston, MA: Intercultural Press, 1994).

Phase Two: Expanding Cultural Awareness and Cultivating Spiritual Transformation

1. Eric H. F. Law, *Who Am I?* Kaleidoscope Institute, Los Angeles, CA. Video uploaded to YouTube, March 26, 2008. <http://www.youtube.com/watch?v=lP_Ia0Zitd

2. Marshall Rosenberg, *Nonviolent Communication: A Language of Life* (Encinitas, CA: Puddledancer Press, 2003), 149–52.

3. Eric H. F. Law, *The Wolf Shall Dwell with the Lamb: A Spirituality for Leadership in a Multicultural Community* (St. Louis, MO: Chalice Press, 1993), 82–88.

4. Thomas Porter, *The Spirit and Art of Conflict Transformation: Creating a Culture of JustPeace* (Nashville, TN: Upper Room Books, 2010), 75–88.

5. Eckhart Tolle, *The Power of Now: A Guide to Spiritual Enlightenment* (Novato, CA: New World Library, 1999), 38.

6. Herbert Benson and Miriam Z. Klipper, *The Relaxation Response* (New York, NY: HarperTorch, 1975), 159–66.

7. Philip Caraman, *Ignatious Loyola: A Biography of the Founder of the Jesuits* (San Francisco, CA: HarperCollins, 1990), 41.

8. Siang-Yang Tan and Douglas H. Gregg, *Disciplines of the Holy Spirit: How to Connect to the Spirit's Power and Presence* (Grand Rapids, MI: Zondervan, 1997), 60.

9. Jon Kabat-Zinn, *Wherever You Go, There You Are: Mindfulness Meditation in Everyday Life* (New York: Hyperion, 1994), 3.

10. Ron Delbene, Mary Montgomery, and Herb Montgomery, *The Breath of Life: A Simple Way to Pray* (Eugene, OR: Wipf and Stock, 2005), 39–42.

BEFORE the Mission Experience

1. Rosenberg, *Nonviolent Communication*, 149–52.

2. Ibid.

3. Adapted from the *Team Leader Handbook* produced by Southeastern Jurisdiction UMVIM (2010), 59.

4. Ibid., 61.

5. *UMVIM Training Manual for Mission Volunteers* (United Methodist General Board of Global Ministries, 2005), 21, 197.

6. *UMVIM Handbook for United Methodist Volunteers in Mission* (Southeastern Jurisdiction Office of Coordination, 2005), 60–61.

DURING the Mission Experience

1. *The Book of Discipline*, 91, ¶120.

2. Rosenberg, *Nonviolent Communication*, 52–55.

3. Ibid., 141–44.

4. *UMVIM Training Manual for Mission Volunteers*, 35–37.

5. Ibid.

6. Ibid.

AFTER the Mission Experience

1. Nicholas Thomas Wright, *How God Became King: The Forgotten Story of the Gospels* (New York: HarperCollins, 2012), 242.

2. Ibid., 145.

3. John L. Epps, ed., *Bending History: Selected Talks of Joseph Wesley Mathews* (Lutz, FL: Resurgence Publishing Corporation, 2005).

4. Ibid., 143–45.

5. Stephen C. Ives, telephone conversation, May 13, 2013.

6. Cami Walker, *29 Gifts: How a Month of Giving Can Change Your Life* (Philadelphia, PA: De Capo, 2009), 14–15.

7. Kabat-Zinn, *Wherever You Go, There You Are*, xiv.

8. Thomas Merton, *New Seeds of Contemplation* (New York, NY: New Directions Publishing Corporation, 2007), 224.

9. Stephen Schwartz, "Day by Day" (from the musical *Godspell*), 1971.

10. Desmond Tutu, *No Future Without Forgiveness*, (New York, NY: Doubleday, 2000), 31.

11. Chad Hall, "Missional Possible: Steps to transform a consumer church into a missional church," *Leadership Journal*, http://www.christianitytoday.com/le/2007/winter/2.34.html?start=2#comments (accessed October 17, 2013).

12. Alan and Debra Hirsch, *Untamed: Reactivating a Missional Form of Discipleship* (Grand Rapids, MI: Baker Publishing Company, 2010), 24.

13. Lisa Shirch, *The Little Book of Strategic Peacebuilding: A vision and framework for peace and justice* (Intercourse, PA: Good Books, 2004), 24.

14. Tutu, *No Future Without Forgiveness*, 265.

APPENDIX

THE MISSION THEOLOGY STATEMENT GUIDES GLOBAL MINISTRIES' PARTICIPATION IN THE MISSIO DEI.

It frames Global Ministries' role within the denominational mission to *make disciples of Jesus Christ for the transformation of the world*. The transforming power belongs to God, and Global Ministries is in mission to witness to what God has done and is doing, and to learn from what God is doing in every land where disciples gather in the name of Jesus Christ.

GOD'S MISSION FROM CREATION TO COMPLETION

God's mission reclaims the life of all creatures and redeems all creation for God's intended purpose. Holy scripture bears witness to mission that begins with God, belongs to God, and will be fulfilled by God at the end of time. The Spirit of God, which moved over the waters of chaos at creation, and the Word of God, which became incarnate in Jesus Christ, leads on to fullness in God's purpose.

THE SELF-EMPTYING LIFE OF JESUS THE CHRIST IN SERVICE TO THE LEAST AND THE LAST

In response to God's mission for him, Jesus—whom we Christians acknowledge as God's son, the Christ, the anointed servant of God, and our savior—poured himself out in servanthood for all humanity and emptied himself of divine privilege, assuming the trials and risks of human limitation. Jesus identified in compassion with all humanity and lived in radical faithfulness to the will of God. He became obedient unto death—even a humiliating public execution. In raising Jesus from the dead, God shows willingness and power to reconcile all creation and to restore the world to its divine purpose.

THE CHURCH AS A COMMUNITY OF SERVANTHOOD IN MISSION

God's Holy Spirit calls the church into being for mission. The church is one sign of God's presence in the world and of God's intention for creation. In response to God's call and the leading of the Holy Spirit, women and men, young and old, of all nations, stations, and races, and in all times and places, unite as the living body of Christ to join God's mission of redemption, bearing witness to God's presence in the world. This community of faith aspires to live out the potential of new life in Christ among all human beings now, while envisioning the fulfillment of God's reign and the completion of God's mission. The church experiences and engages in God's mission as it pours itself out for others, ready to cross every boundary to call for true human dignity among all peoples, especially among those regarded as the least of God's children, all the while making disciples of Christ for the transformation of the world.

GRACE AT WORK EVERYWHERE

In our Wesleyan tradition we acknowledge the grace of God placed in our hearts and at work in the world before any action on our part. In response, we accept and proclaim grace that sets us upon the right path of obedience to the Word made flesh in Jesus Christ. This grace calls us to repentance, and to active faith and good works in Christ. Active faith participates in the perfecting and fulfilling grace of God, which claims and implements the promises of God to deliver exploited persons and oppressed peoples, to restore the sanctity and integrity of God's creation, and to reconcile division in the households of faith and among the peoples and nations of the earth as all of creation groans for redemption. The Wesleyan expectation of "perfection in love" draws redeemed individuals into appropriate, active, transforming relationships of wholeness and unity with God, all people, and creation. Repentance and faith elicit both personal salvation, and social and cosmic transformation.

TRANSFORMATIVE WITNESS

The church in mission lifts up the name of Jesus in thought, word, and deed, proclaiming Jesus Christ as "the Word become flesh" through its own incarnate living; deeds of love; and service, healing, and renewal. By representing the revelation of God in Christ in word and deed, the church remains faithful both to the Great Commandment that we love God with all our heart, soul, mind, and strength, and our neighbor as ourselves; and to the Great Commission that we make disciples of all nations. The church as faithful community moves full of hope toward the transformation of the world and the day when God's mission is fulfilled.

GOD'S PRIOR PRESENCE, OUR CURRENT RESPONSE

God's light shines in every corner of the earth, and God's mission extends to all creation. There are no places where God's grace has not always been present, only places where God in Christ is not recognized, served, or heeded. Because God's image is present in every human being throughout the world, mission partnership embraces witness in all cultures, traditions, political arrangements, economic structures, and languages. Partners in God's mission seek to hear God's voice, to discover the signs of the moving of the Spirit through the world today, and to bear witness to God's activity—overarching past, present, and future—in every local setting.

THE SPIRIT'S SURPRISING ACTIVITY

The Spirit is always moving to sweep the church into a new mission age. With openness and gratitude we await the leading of the Spirit in ways not yet seen as God continues to work God's purposes out in our own day in a new way.

BEST PRACTICES FOR UMVIM/VIM (SENDING AND HOSTING) TEAMS

1. Preparation and planning should take place at least a year in advance.
2. Mission volunteer journeys should be accompanied with a formal invitation from the host that includes approval from the local head of church.
3. Team leaders should be UMVIM-trained and have volunteer mission journey experience prior to leading a team.
4. Communications and all budgeting/funding should be fully transparent to the sending and hosting team leaders.
5. Team leaders should advise their own Annual Conference UMVIM Coordinator and their UMVIM Jurisdictional Coordinator of the journey.
6. Hosting teams should set the tone and directions, providing clear expectations for the UMVIM team. Sending teams should respect the host's direction and work to build mutual respect.
7. All team members should follow Safe Sanctuary and child/adult protection guidelines.
8. Medical and accident insurance should be obtained for each team member. Hosting partners are encouraged to require it for all teams.
9. Team members should not interfere in any local church ministries or politics.
10. Devotional times, debriefing, and evaluations should be shared opportunities that include the host leader and host team members whenever appropriate.

UNITED METHODIST COMMITTEE ON RELIEF (UMCOR) VOLUNTEERS AND US RESPONSE TO DISASTER

Greg Forrester, Assistant General Secretary for US Disaster Response (UMCOR)

The United Methodist Committee on Relief (UMCOR) provides humanitarian relief in the United States. Our efforts are targeted at places where natural disasters, man-made disasters, or economic conditions have done so much damage that communities are unable to recover on their own. While UMCOR is not a first-response organization, it stands ready to accompany communities in need over the long haul of their recovery, until they are well on their way to establishing a "new normal" after a crisis.

UMCOR HELPS

1. Prepare for disasters. UMCOR works cooperatively with annual conferences in the event of an emergency and to prepare for emergencies. UMCOR works through the annual conference to provide training in all aspects of disaster response. Call your United Methodist conference office for the name of your disaster response coordinator and United Methodist Volunteers In Mission (UMVIM) coordinator.

2. Respond to disasters. UMCOR always responds to emergencies at the invitation of and through the affected annual conference. In addition to providing training, UMCOR offers technical assistance and support through a highly trained network of staff, consultants, and experienced volunteers to help annual conferences respond to all phases of a disaster.

3. Recover from disasters. UMCOR can send emergency grants immediately to fund start-up relief activities. UMCOR also supports long-term recovery ministries through the provision of grants, planning, material resources, public relations, technical assistance, Christian care/counseling, case management training, and helps coordinate volunteers. All requests for assistance are received through the conference disaster coordinator.

All three of these areas require dedicated and trained volunteers.

EARLY STAGES FOLLOWING A DISASTER

When a disaster strikes in an annual conference, the Disaster Response Coordinator (DRC) connects with United Methodist churches within the affected area. Depending on the scope of the disaster, additional resources beyond the local church congregation may be required. Often, the disaster can be handled locally. The DRC may request Early Response Teams (ERTs) to come to the affected area. If this occurs, the conference UMVIM coordinator should also be notified as part of the conference disaster-response plan. ERTs usually respond within the first two to four weeks of a disaster and only on invitation from the DRC.

Early Response Teams are specialized volunteer in mission teams. Members of an ERT attend a training program offered by accredited UMCOR trainers, undergo a background check, and are then issued a badge indicating affiliation and training. ERTs are primarily used to respond to disasters within their own annual conference, but if an annual conference experiences a large-scale disaster it may request additional support from ERTs from other areas by contacting the UMVIM Jurisdictional office. ERT leaders should receive UMVIM Team Leader Training.

LONG-TERM RECOVERY

A community affected by disaster will not recover without the assistance of voluntary agencies. The United Methodist Church, through UMCOR, is a member of National Voluntary Organizations Active in Disaster (www.NVOAD.org). The organization is comprised of both secular and faith-based organizations that come together to provide a holistic approach to disaster recovery.

The affected community is responsible for its own recovery process. Community members are encouraged to form regional Long-Term Recovery Committees (LTRCs) and United Methodist churches in the region should have representation at the LTRC. UMCOR brings its expertise and funding to the annual conference and to the LTRC through local United Methodist representation. It is crucial that local United Methodist churches respond to disasters within their geographic presence.

UMVIM teams become a required part of the sequence of recovery for members of the affected community. In the majority of disasters, community recovery involves the extensive participation of volunteers. UMCOR assists the annual conference to develop a calendaring and hosting system for UMVIM teams.

PREPARATION FOR VOLUNTEERS

1. Become a badged ERT member and get active in your local or district Early Response Team.
2. Receive additional training from your local Red Cross so you are ready to assist during or immediately following a disaster. The Federal Emergency Management Agency (FEMA) also offers some excellent online courses.
3. Become trained as a UMVIM team leader, conference Care Team member, Stephen Minister, or another specialty so you are ready to respond when disaster strikes.

UNITED METHODIST COMMITTEE ON RELIEF (UMCOR) VOLUNTEERS AND INTERNATIONAL DISASTER RESPONSE

Jack Amick, Assistant General Secretary for International Disaster Response

When disaster strikes in distant countries and news media flood with images of suffering, our human instinct—and our duty as Christians—is to reach out with compassion. Many of us are motivated to give and pray, but some of us are compelled to go. We want to be present, to heal and connect, as Christ did, with those who are experiencing loss and brokenness. "Why can't I go?" we ask.

A common misunderstanding about UMCOR's International Disaster Response is that we have a team of people who will "parachute" into a disaster zone immediately after the tragedy. That isn't the case. UMCOR does not engage in rescue operations. Local authorities and trained emergency-response professionals perform this function.

EARLY STAGES FOLLOWING A DISASTER

As soon as possible after a disaster, UMCOR responds with emergency relief, providing food, water, shelter—whatever is most needed in the particular situation. When possible, we use local or international partner organizations already situated in the country, or in some cases, local volunteers or UMCOR staff, to advise us of the needs and establish a distribution system for these materials. Sometimes this assistance includes items such as health kits prepared by United Methodist churches in the United States and stored at and shipped from one of our relief-supply depots.

In the weeks after a disaster, UMCOR continues to evaluate the situation, with assistance from our local contacts and partners, to develop a long-term strategy. Our goal is to determine whether there is a specific role that UMCOR could play in meeting the needs of those who are suffering from the disaster. In the emergency relief and early recovery phases of the disaster, UMCOR works with one or more partners to fill a particular gap in the lives of those affected.

BEST WAYS TO HELP

In the early stages of disaster response, volunteers are most helpful by staying at home and mobilizing support for UMCOR's efforts. Conducting fund-raising events, offering congregations specific items and issues about which to pray, organizing volunteers to assemble health kits and other kits (as specified on the UMCOR website), working with clergy and worship committees to design opportunities for the community to come together in worship, organizing a "Go with Our Hearts" mission journey (in which participants spend a week or weekend at their home church learning about the affected country, assembling kits, worshiping, and raising awareness in the community) are all wonderful ways for leaders of volunteers to use their leadership skills and passion in response to an international disaster.

CAUTIONS

"Why can't I go?" we might still ask. Sending volunteers, even trained UMVIM leaders, into countries suffering from disaster often results in more harm than good. John Wesley's advice to "do no harm" is good guidance. When volunteers inject themselves into a disaster situation, the infrastructure already under stress becomes further strained. We would do best to leave the limited resources of food, water, transportation, and lodging to the experts—local and international.

Similarly, shipping used clothing, food, and old medicine usually results in logistical headaches for local disaster managers and sometimes rotting piles of materials. Congregations and individuals are instead urged to consult the UMCOR website for guidance in assembling relief kits and sending these to any of the eight depots in the UMCOR Relief-Supply Network.

LONG-TERM VOLUNTEER OPTIONS

Later, when UMCOR and other agencies begin to tackle long-term development challenges such as water and sanitation, food security, housing and infrastructure, employment generation, and other issues, there may be opportunities for UMVIM leaders to explore options for UMVIM teams with local Methodist leaders. UMVIM Jurisdictional Coordinators are positioned best to provide accurate information about prospective opportunities and journeys.

When the impulse is to get on an airplane and go, it may be hard to wait, but finding other ways to be a part of the United Methodist connection of caring is the best gift volunteers can offer in the face of an international disaster. Pray, give, reach out, connect, but don't go . . . not just yet.

UNITED METHODIST COMMITTEE ON RELIEF (UMCOR) GLOBAL HEALTH AND MISSION VOLUNTEERS

Shannon Trilli, Director of UMCOR Global Health

Since the 2008 General Conference, global health has been a significant area of focus for The United Methodist Church. Accompanying our brothers and sisters in communities around the world to access, learn about, and find their own solutions to care and holistic health is a powerful way for mission volunteers to serve.

The Imagine No Malaria Initiative (INM) was the first iteration of our church's global health strategy, working with UMC Central Conferences in Africa to address malaria throughout our vast United Methodist health system on the continent. A central strategy of INM was to work with each African Central Conference to establish health boards. Initially the role of the health board was to provide a structure of governance, finance, and accountability and to implement the funds raised through INM in a way that was transparent and demonstrated impact. In addition to organizing programs with INM funds, the health boards in Africa are charged with health experts and leaders that define and implement the health priorities for the local church beyond malaria. The health boards prioritize health areas like maternal survival, child health, or access to clean water. The health boards also oversee UMC health facilities within the local annual conference.

POINT OF CONTACT

When planning a health-related mission journey, *even if you have your own local contact*, the first piece of advice for mission volunteers is to contact and work through your United Methodist Volunteers In Mission (UMVIM) Jurisdictional Coordinator and Health Care Volunteers Blog (www.umvim4health.blogspot.com) who will assist in contacting the appropriate *episcopal office and local health board* (contact/coordinator). The health board coordinator (or person in a similar role) will be able to assist the UMVIM team's travel logistics, ensure that all requisite certifications to practice medicine or enter the country are met, serve as a liaison to the bishop's office and local church, and be a point of contact, context, and accountability for the team while in the country. In addition to having health board coordinators for the United Methodist churches in Africa, UMCOR has worked with Methodist partners in Haiti and Colombia, and aims to expand the health board model, adapting it to other key countries.

RESOURCES AVAILABLE FOR A MEDICAL TEAM

The UMVIM Jurisdictional Coordinators/Health Care Volunteers Blog (www.umvim4health.blogspot.com) contains a host of specific information for all health-related mission teams, and team leaders are encouraged to use their many resources. For example, UMVIM medical teams need to forward credentials (for instance, their medical license) to the country's Ministry of Health or other approving agency prior to service. This is often a lengthy bureaucratic process, and team leaders need to plan ahead of time for this one aspect of a health-related mission journey.

SEEK TO TEACH AND LEARN, NOT JUST PRACTICE

While many communities and patients can benefit from the skills of a medical mission team for longer-term impact, UMCOR encourages medical or health-related mission teams to aim to learn from and empower their new colleagues and friends in the local place of mission. This will ensure that the impact of the mission extends beyond the journey time line. More importantly, work side by side with other professionals in the country during your term of mission service, learning from one another and developing a relationship of respect as you go.

LOOKING FOR A MEDICAL MISSION OPPORTUNITY?

For a team looking for a medical mission opportunity (see UMVIM/Health Care Volunteers Blog at www.umvim4health.blogspot.com), UMCOR can help the team connect with a health board. Health volunteer opportunities are currently divided into two categories: (1) medical mission teams that provide general medicine or even surgery to recipient communities, and (2) health board capacity building, which includes helping health boards or health facilities in the development of "soft" skills that will further the church's health ministry. Volunteers who sign up for health board capacity building projects will assist partners in activities like strategic planning, developing a budget for a project, learning to use Excel or QuickBooks, and so on. UMCOR Health currently works with the health boards to fill out the UMVIM request forms, and it is a resource to volunteer teams looking for health or medical opportunities.

The Global Ministries' Individual Volunteers program offers medical mission training events throughout the year in the five UMC jurisdictions. These mandatory trainings for Individual Volunteer Service provide opportunities to learn more and be better prepared. Please visit www.individualvolunteers.info for more information. Contact us at www.umvim4health.blogspot.com or umcor@umcor.org if you have questions.

IN MISSION TOGETHER: 50/50 PARTNERSHIP COVENANT

Patrick Friday, Director of In Mission Together

LONG-TERM PARTNERSHIP FOR LONG-TERM IMPACT

What are your next steps in developing a long-term relationship with your partner? How can your ministry or project have long-term impact? The In Mission Together (IMT) global partnership network was created to address both of these questions by equipping your team, conference, district, or church for long-term transformational partnerships in the United States and around the world.

Whereas needs-based, short-term relief is the most common approach to mission engagement, the In Mission Together vision of partnership focuses on asset-based, long-term development. IMT partners commit to one another through the 50/50 Partnership Covenant to participate equally, 50/50, as the body of Christ in holistic ministry. This is an important step in the process because the 50/50 framework was designed to prevent dependency and foster self-sufficiency. It addresses systemic issues rather than treating symptoms alone. The covenant was designed for partners who are committed to developing The United Methodist Church globally.

We encourage you to have a day-one conversation with your mission partner based on the IMT 50/50 Partnership Covenant. It is a simple, straightforward tool that enables you to be more effective, do no harm, empower others, and have long-term impact. It is based on best practices gathered from the Mission Initiatives of The United Methodist Church. It provides you with a framework for partnership that serves as a catalyst for collaboration. The 50/50 Covenant fosters an asset-based approach through our five core values: church planting, spiritual formation, community development, communication through social networking, preventing dependency, and promoting self-sufficiency—for example, how would the following principle affect how you engage in mission together?

The partners set aside their own agendas and create a collective vision for the ministry or project together. As with any relationship, each participant brings their God-given gifts, whether spiritual, physical or mental, tangible or intangible, which will be honored and appreciated equally—50/50.

Another principle from the covenant encourages restraint on the part of the outside partner to create space for the local partner who lives in the community and has ownership of the vision for the ministry or project. *We pledge not to do for the other what they can do for themselves. We gladly serve one another as Christ has served us—with humility, love and encouragement, building a strong foundation for ministry together.*

In Mission Together is "glocal" (both global and local) and equips you for cross-cultural ministry in a variety of contexts. Our team of IMT Partnership Coordinators is available to assist you in the development of a 50/50 partnership.

For more information on IMT and the Covenant, please visit our website at www.inmissiontogether.org.

PARTNERSHIP COVENANT 50/50

The Covenant—Description & Pledge

Please read *1 Corinthians 12:12-31* and discuss the following:

The purpose of an In Mission Together (IMT) partnership is to develop a healthy relationship between brothers and sisters in Christ across cultures through God's grace that is transformative and inspirational.

The IMT program equips, facilitates, and resources you and your church in developing a collaborative partnership which builds strong relationships over the long-term and enables you to share in the historic development of a mission of The United Methodist Church.

The goal of the IMT program is to have honest and open interaction with your partner, carefully listening to one another as equal parts of the body of Christ. It's a sacred covenant between recipient and donor to support one another and participate equally and proportionally—50/50—in a ministry or project.

The goal of the mission is the establishment of a self-sustaining United Methodist Church with holistic ministries empowering people in their context, community, and country.

The partners set aside their own agendas and create a collective vision for the ministry or project together. As with any relationship, each participant brings God-given gifts, whether spiritual, physical or mental, tangible or intangible, that will be honored and appreciated equally—50/50—in the covenant agreement.

This round table of listeners and learners embarks on a journey with a vision for the mission as a whole with God's help focusing not simply on the task at hand, but on the more significant impact of building strong relationships, empowering local people to improve their lives and develop their church.

We pledge not to do for the other what they can do for themselves. We gladly serve each other as Christ has served us, with humility, love and encouragement, building a strong foundation for the ministry together.

We create mutual accountability and transparency through patiently engaging one another. We will be flexible and adaptable enabling both partners to span language and culture through God's guidance.

The ownership of the ministry or project rests not with the donor, but the recipient. They are the leaders called by God to nurture the church in their community. The donors are "working themselves out of a job," seeking neither credit nor control, and all partners are sharing in the blessing of a job well done together!

Please acknowledge your agreement with the covenant by your signature(s):

For more information, visit www.inmissiontogether.org.

UNITED METHODIST COMMUNICATIONS (UMCOM) UNDERSTANDING INFORMATION AND COMMUNICATIONS TECHNOLOGY IN THE DEVELOPING WORLD

N. Neelley Hicks, Director of ICT4D Church Initiatives

Information and communications technology is part of daily life for those of us in the "developed" world. When traveling into rural parts of developing countries, you will find great poverty, not just in material things but also in information itself. United Methodist Communications is working to bridge this gap through innovative technologies built specifically for low-resource environments through its ICT4D (Information and Communications Technology for Development) Church Initiatives. UMCOM can connect your team with the best in global practitioners, tested technology, and training in innovations so that all facets of ministry are enhanced through better communications.

This document is intended to facilitate necessary communications for your mission team and empower you to be part of the bridge-building efforts to twenty-first-century communications.

HOW WILL MY MISSION TEAM COMMUNICATE WHILE AWAY?

Before you leave, purchase an unlocked GSM phone (which are quite inexpensive) for your travels. Once you have arrived, purchase a SIM card (often found through street vendors) that will allow you to call and text your team while in the country. You will also be able to send international texts (fees vary based on mobile carrier).

HOW WILL MY MISSION TEAM KEEP THOSE BACK HOME UPDATED?

While you can expect low bandwidth or no bandwidth in a majority of settings in the developing world, there are a few tricks of the trade that can help. When you purchase your in-country SIM card, be sure that it contains both voice and data capacity. biNu (www.binu.com) provides access to basic phones that have Internet access so you can post to Facebook and Twitter while away. A GSM modem/dongle can link your computer to data coverage by placing the same SIM card into it and connecting to a USB port. These modems can be purchased locally or online through shop.umc.org.

ACCESS TO ELECTRICITY

Electricity can be unreliable or nonexistent in many areas abroad. Staying in touch with others in-country and at home requires charging your cell phone. While there are solar options available online for your team, you may also want to consider in-country purchases that can be left behind for those with whom you are in ministry. UMCOM can provide recommendations and contacts for you. If you are planning a mission that requires use of electrical equipment, UMCOM can provide you with recommendations for alternative power supplies.

PREVENTING VIRUSES

If you are planning to take your laptop and share files with others, you will need to take extra precaution in virus protection. UMCOM recommends using SD cards with SD card readers (as opposed to flash drives). The SD cards can receive files from your computer. They can become read-only when transferring files to another computer. Simply slide the Read/Write tab on the card before transferring. Deep Freeze software can be added to your system making it possible to reset your computer to previous settings so that it is protected from infection.

HARDWARE

Some hardware withstands power fluctuations, high temperatures, dust, water, and falls better than others, so be careful in what you bring. UMCOM has tested tablets, laptops, desktops, and projectors for rugged conditions and now offers certified solutions through The United Methodist Church e-store (shop.umc.org). Laptops are available with batteries lasting seven to nine hours and use only ten watts of power. You are likely to have greater success using equipment that is built for rugged conditions than with computers and other electronics built for air-conditioned, high-resource settings.

SOFTWARE

FrontlineSMS is a free downloadable software that can be used for group communications in settings where there is no Internet. All that is required is a computer, software, an unlocked GSM modem, and a voice SIM card. Mobile numbers can be added to its database to send group messages to your team. Depending on the mission, number of volunteers, and worksites, this software may be invaluable to the team's leader in reaching a group without one-by-one entry. For more information, visit www.frontlinesms.com.

BUILDING COMMUNICATIONS INFRASTRUCTURE

Whether you are participating in educational, medical, evangelistic, or other ministries, you will notice a gap in the means of transmitting communications available to workers. Mobile phones can be maximized to make a lasting difference in a community by pairing with software and other appropriate ultra-low power technologies.

While you are there, talk with local leaders to learn how they share information among those in the community, report to other leaders, and provide critical messages about health, weather, and the like. Take good notes, and follow up with the UMCOM ICT4D Church Initiatives program. With more innovative solutions available—and even more on the horizon—you can be a part of building a bridge to twenty-first-century communications that enhances and even saves lives.

For more information, visit www.umcom.org/global, or contact Neelley Hicks, 615-742-5400, nhicks@umcom.org.

ADDITIONAL RECOMMENDED RESOURCES

Understanding the Theology of Christian Mission

A Mile in My Shoes: Cultivating Compassion by Trevor Hudson (Nashville, TN: Upper Room Books, 2005).

Called to Be Sent: Co-missioned as Disciples Today by Anthony Gittins (Ligouri, MO: Liguori Publications, 2008).

Change the World: Recovering the Message and Mission of Jesus by Mike Slaughter (Nashville, TN: Abingdon, 2010).

Getting Ready to Come Back: An Advocacy Guide for Mission Teams by Beth Reilly (Washington, DC: Bread for the World, 2009).

Mission in the 21st Century: Exploring the Five Marks of Global Mission by Andrew F. Walls and Cathy Ross (Maryknoll, NY: Orbis, 2008).

The Hole in Our Gospel: What Does God Expect of Us? by Richard Sterns (Nashville, TN: Thomas Nelson, 2009).

The Mission of God's People: A Biblical Theology of the Church's Mission by Christopher J. H. Wright (Grand Rapids, MI: Zondervan, 2010).

Toxic Charity: How Churches and Charities Hurt Those They Help (And How to Reverse It) by Robert D. Lupton (New York, NY: HarperCollins, 2011).

When Helping Hurts: How to Alleviate Poverty without Hurting the Poor . . . and Yourself by Steve Corbett and Brian Fikkert (Chicago, IL: Moody Publishers, 2009).

Expanding Cultural Sensitivity

Cross-Cultural Dialogues: 74 Brief Encounters with Cultural Difference by Craig Storti (Boston, MA: Intercultural Press, 1994).

Embracing the World: Faith, Hope, Love in Action by Jay Godfrey (Women's Division, The General Board of Global Ministries of The United Methodist Church, 2010).

Foreign to Familiar: A Guide to Understanding Hot- and Cold-Climate Cultures by Sarah A. Lanier (Hagerstown, MD: McDougal Publishing, 2000).

Ministering Cross-Culturally, An Incarnational Model for Personal Relationships by Sherwood G. Lingenfelter and Marvin K. Mayers (Grand Rapids, MI: Baker Academic, 2003).

Ministry at the Margins: Strategy and Spirituality for Missions by Anthony Gittins (New York, NY: Orbis, 2002).

Mutuality in Mission by Glory and Jacob Dharmaraj (General Board of Global Ministries of The United Methodist Church, 2001).

Serving with Eyes Wide Open: Doing Short-Term Missions with Cultural Intelligence by David A. Livermore (Grand Rapids, MI: Baker, 2006).

Short-Term Missions Workbook, from Mission Tourists to Global Citizens by Tim Dearborn (Downers Grove, IL: InterVarsity, 2003).

Survival Kit for Overseas Living: For Americans Planning to Live and Work Abroad, fourth ed., by Robert L. Kohls (Yarmouth, ME: Nicholas Brealey Publishing, 2001).

The Wolf Shall Dwell with the Lamb: A Spirituality for Leadership in a Multicultural Community by Eric H. F. Law (St. Louis, MO: Chalice Press, 1993).

Toxic Charity: How Churches and Charities Hurt Those They Help (And How to Reverse It) by Robert D. Lupton (New York, NY: HarperCollins, 2011).

When Helping Hurts: How to Alleviate Poverty Without Hurting the Poor . . . and Yourself by Steve Corbett, and Brian Fikkert (Chicago, IL: Moody Publishers, 2009).

Cultivating Spiritual Transformation

Can You Drink the Cup? by Henri J. M. Nouwen (Notre Dame, IN: Ave Maria Press, 1996).

Chicken Soup for the Volunteer's Soul: Stories to Celebrate the Spirit of Courage, Caring, and Community by Jack Canfield, Mark Victor Hansen, Arline McGraw Oberst, John T. Boal, Tom Lagana, and Laura Lagana (Deerfield Beach, FL: Health Communications Inc., 2002).

Gracias! A Latin American Journal by Henri J. M. Nouwen (New York, NY: Harper & Row, 1987).

Life of the Beloved: Spiritual Living in a Secular World by Henri J. M. Nouwen (New York, NY: Crossroad Publishing Company, 1992).

Living the Message: Daily Reflections with Eugene Peterson by Eugene Petersen (New York, NY: HarperCollins, 1996).

Meeting God in the Ruins: Devotions for Disaster Volunteers, edited by Beth Ann Gaede (Evangelical Lutheran Church in America, 2008).

Nonviolent Communication: A Language of Life by Marshall Rosenberg (Encinitas, CA: Puddledancer Press, 2003).

The Breath of Life: A Simple Way to Pray by Ron DelBene with Mary and Herb Montgomery (Eugene, OR: Wipf and Stock, 2005).

The Little Book of Circle Processes: A New/Old Approach to Peacemaking by Kay Pranis (Intercourse, PA: Good Books, 2005).

The Wolf Shall Dwell with the Lamb: A Spirituality for Leadership in a Multicultural Community by Eric H. F. Law (St. Louis, MO: Chalice Press, 1993).

The Wounded Healer by Henri J. M. Nouwen (New York, NY: Doubleday, 1990).

Transforming Ventures: A Spiritual Guide for Volunteers in Mission by Jane P. Ives (Nashville, TN: Upper Room Books, 2000).

Learning More about Peace and Justice

No Future Without Forgiveness by Desmond Tutu (New York, NY: Doubleday, 1992).

Speak Peace in a World of Conflict: What You Say Next Will Change Your World by Marshall Rosenberg (Encinitas, CA: Puddledancer Press, 2005).

The Little Books of Justice & Peacebuilding, produced by the Center for Justice and Peacebuilding of Eastern Mennonite University in cooperation with Good Books.

The Little Book of Strategic Peacebuilding by Lisa Shirch (Intercourse, PA: Good Books, 2004).

The Spirit and Art of Conflict Transformation by Thomas Porter (Nashville, TN: Upper Room Books, 2010).